The Secret for Teens Revealed

THE SECRET FOR TEENS REVEALED

How Parents, Teachers, and Teenagers Can Inspire Leadership and Transform Lives

ANDREA SAMADI

Foreword by Bob Proctor
Teacher from the movie **The Secret**

The material in this guide, when properly studied and applied,
is guaranteed to change the course of your life.

The Secret for Teens Revealed: How Parents, Teachers, and Teenagers Can Inspire Leadership and Transform Lives

Published by Wheatmark®
610 East Delano Street, Suite 104
Tucson, Arizona 85705 U.S.A.
www.wheatmark.com

International Standard Book Number: 978-1-60494-033-6
Library of Congress Control Number: 2008928203

This book is dedicated to my husband, Majid Samadi, who continues to inspire and motivate me on a daily basis with his own personal achievements. I will be forever grateful for his knowledge, his adventurous spirit, and his desire to learn.

Contents

Preface: The Author Reveals the Secret xi
History and Testimonials. xix
Now It's Your Turn to Study xxiii
Foreword. xxvii
Introduction and Purpose Behind This Study Guide 1
How to Use This Study Guide. 2
Personal Inventory for Parents, Teachers, and Teenagers 9

Understanding Your Learning Styles

Think About This! 21
Lesson. 22
Learning Styles and Multiple Intelligences. 23
Multiple Intelligences Test. 27
Follow-up with the Multiple Intelligence Theory 38

Ten Top-Secret Lessons

Test Your Current Knowledge on Attitude 45
**Lesson 1: Why is a winning attitude so important for a
rewarding life?**. **49**

Think About This! 50
Lesson. 51
Review 54
Extension Exercises 60

Test Your Current Knowledge of the Mind 64
**Lesson 2: What is your mind, and how does it control your
destiny?** **66**

Think About This! 67
Review 69

Extension Exercise. 70

Lessons on the Mind 71

Review 85

Extension Exercises 86

Test Your Current Knowledge of the Laws of the Universe 87

Lesson 3: How will the laws of the universe change your life immediately? **89**

Think About This! 90

Lessons 91

Test Your Current Knowledge of Goal Setting. 107

Lesson 4: How does goal setting and persistence set you apart from all others? **109**

Think About This! 110

Lesson. 112

Review 116

Extension Exercise: My 101 Goals. 119

Test Your Current Knowledge of Persistence 123

Think About This! 125

Lesson. 126

Extension Exercises 128

Test Your Current Knowledge of Confidence. 132

Lesson 5: How can the confidence formula and body image give you predictable results for success?. **135**

Think About This! 136

Lesson. 137

Review 139

Extension Exercises 142

Review 145

Extension Exercise. 146

Test Your Current Knowledge of Responsibility 147

Lesson 6: Why will responsibility shape your future? **150**

Think About This! 151

Lesson: How Responsible Decisions Will Affect Your Life 152

Review 160
Extension Exercises 162

Test Your Current Knowledge of Your Habits and Beliefs. 164

Lesson 7: How can you turn your life around by blasting through things that make you nervous?. 168

Think About This! 169
Prepare 170
Lesson 171
Review 173
Extension Exercise. 175
Lesson 176

Test Your Current Knowledge of Self-Motivation, Values, Integrity, and Self-Image 181

Lesson 8: How do self-motivation and your values help you live a decent life of integrity? 183

Think About This! 184
Lesson 185
Review 191
Extension Exercise. 193
Test Your Current Knowledge of Self-Image 195
Think About This! 197
Lesson 198
Review 200
Extension Exercises 202

Test Your Current Knowledge of Courage. 204

Lesson 9: How can you let your courage emerge from within and rocket your life?. 206

Think About This! 207
Lesson 208
Review 210
Extension Exercise. 211
Visualize Your Dreams. 213
Lesson 214
Review 216
Extension Exercise. 218

Test Your Current Knowledge of What You Want to Do with the Rest of Your Life . . 219

Lesson 10: What difference will you make in your lifetime? **221**

Think About This! 222
Lesson 223
Review 226
Extension Exercises 227

Putting it All Together:
A Master Plan for a Better Life

Prepare 231
Think About This! 232
Lesson 1: Attitude 233
Lesson 2: Your Mind and the Six Higher Faculties 234
Lesson 3: The Laws of the Universe 235
Lesson 4: Goal Setting and Persistence 236
Lesson 5: Confidence 238
Lesson 6: Responsibility 239
Lesson 7: Understanding Your Paradigms, or Habits 240
Lesson 8: Self-Motivation, Your Values, and Self-Image 241
Lesson 9: Courage 242
Lesson Ten: What Difference Will You Make in Your Lifetime? 244

Congratulations on Completing
THE SECRET FOR TEENS REVEALED!

Think About This! 247
Acknowledgments 249
Bibliography 253

Preface: The Author Reveals the Secret

The powerful information you are about to read came together over a twelve-year period of studying with *The Secret*[1] teacher Bob Proctor and many enlightened people who clearly understand the secrets of success. I gathered Proctor's information, added information provided by other teachers who worked closely with him, and finally added my own knowledge to help people to understand this metaphysical material in a more visual manner. In the beginning, I coached some close friends who wanted to understand these abstract yet life-changing ideas to help them make improvements in their lives. Later, I coached teens and young athletes using the same principles and saw them achieve astounding results. It was then that I realized just how powerful the information was, and I knew that I needed to gather as much as I could and record it all in one place.

It was an incredible experience to work so closely with many of these teachers—people who had a positive impact on the world on a daily basis. These truly were exciting times. Each day held adventure and opportunity, and abundance and advancement toward a better life was inevitable. I find it very powerful to look back to see where it all began.

How did I come across this incredible opportunity?

To some, it sounds like it was a simple process. It sounds like I stumbled on this opportunity by chance. I'd been intrigued by a neighbor's exciting life, and I'd noticed that he drove a new car each month. One day in 1996, I simply asked the neighbor, a man named Mark Low, "What do you do for a living?" He didn't say much. Instead,

---

1 Byrne, Rhonda, *The Secret*, DVD (TS Productions LLC, 1996).

he handed me Bob Proctor's book, *You Were Born Rich*,[2] and told me that he was Proctor's director of sales.

While some have said that my good fortune was just luck, I tell them that I was at the right place at the right time, and I was open to a guided learning experience at the hand of another. I later heard a quote by Earl Nightingale. He said, "Luck is when preparation and opportunity meet. If a person is not prepared when the opportunity arises, it will only make them look foolish."

At the time, I didn't know who Bob Proctor was; nor did I know anything about sales or the personal development industry. I would later become a serious student of both. I was a middle school teacher in Toronto, Canada, and I had dreams of changing the world through our educational system. That weekend, I not only read *You Were Born Rich*, I also decided that I wanted to learn more about the incredible potential I knew I had. At the time, it was difficult to locate books that would help me gain a deeper understanding of the information I'd been exposed to. In fact, Rhonda Byrne called the movie she created and produced *The Secret* because many of the avatars and philosophers—Aristotle, Plato, and Dalton—of the past were able to understand this knowledge, but the common person could not. It appeared that these ideas would remain a secret.

I resigned my job as a schoolteacher, and off I went to study. I was interested in hearing about and from anyone who Proctor and his seminar attendees seemed interested in discussing. I devoured every program Proctor had created. I later became a sales representative for Proctor's company, and it was very beneficial to have an understanding of these materials. I started with Proctor's *Success Series* CD program. Since I was aware that there are only two ways to change my old programming, or thinking patterns—through consistent repetition and emotional impact—I knew that if I was able to listen to the CDs for ninety days in a row, I would begin to change my old programming. So off I went to listen to these discs over and over again. In time, my thinking actually started to change, and the concepts I

---

2   Proctor, Bob, *You Were Born Rich* (Scottsdale, AZ: LifeSuccess Productions, 1984).

was learning did not feel so strange or awkward. I also know of people that had a serious emotional impact in their life that affected the way they thought about their future actions. Perhaps a death of a loved one or news of an illness can make one think about the value they place on their life and the direction they will take. I think differently ever time I hear Tim McGraw's song "Live Like You Were Dying"[3] as I realize how precious life is, as it can take me in many different directions that I may or may not ever be able to prepare myself for. Life began to have significant meaning and was starting to be filled with excitement and opportunity.

Next, I studied the *You Were Born Rich*[4] home-study course. During this time, I began to gain a deeper understanding of the talents and abilities within myself. Next, I tackled Proctor's *Success Puzzle*[5] program. This program highlighted areas where I was having problems attaining my goals. Once I realized that my thinking needed to change, my education pertaining to topics I'd chosen to work on became more specialized. I was clearly learning the material, but at this point, learning and doing remained poles apart. I could quote the material word for word, but I was not yet getting results.

My next quest for learning allowed me to discover more about The Laws of the Universe from the *Abraham-Hicks Special Subject Tapes, Vol. 1.*[6] I also was able to move toward Jack Canfield's *Self-Esteem and Peak Performance Program.*[7] I knew I had to change my limiting beliefs, and I knew that this would take time and effort. After mastering the tapes and the program, I was coached by Mark Victor Hansen, author of *Chicken Soup for the Soul.* He personally taught me effective sales strategies while I also learned from his audio program, which is titled *How to Think Bigger than You Ever Thought You Could Think.*[8]

---

3   Tim McGraw, "Live Like You Were Dying," Curb Records, August 2004

4   Proctor, ibid.

5   Proctor, ibid.

6   Hicks, Jerry and Esther, *Special Subjects Volume 1* (San Antonio, TX: Abraham-Hicks Publisher, 1989).

7   Canfield, Jack, *Self-Esteem and Peak Performance*, Audio CD Program (Overland Park, Kansas, CareerTrack, 1990).

8   Hansen, Mark Victor, *How to Think Bigger than You Ever Thought You Could Think* (Provo, UT, Enlightened Millionaire Institute, 2003).

Because I was just learning the sales profession, being trained by these sales experts and winners was very helpful. I even had a recorded phone session with America's number one marketing wizard, Jay Abraham, who wrote *Getting Everything You Can Out of All You've Got.*[9]

As I met more leaders in the motivational speaking industry, I also purchased and implemented their programs. I bought *The Ultimate Speaking Package*[10] from the late Bill Gove. He is still considered the father of public speaking, and this package afforded me a chance to work on my public speaking skills. These skills came in handy years later when I ran my own workshops as a sales representative.

Next, I met Doug Wead, author, humanitarian, and philanthropist, who has written twenty-seven books that have cumulatively sold five million copies and have been translated into thirty languages. As a corporate speaker, he has spoken to audiences on four continents. This incredible leader worked closely with Proctor for some time, and I took it upon myself to make sure I was the one who looked after Wead every time he spoke at Proctor's seminars. To be able to speak with such a world leader is a privilege that most people will never enjoy.

I also met Ron Schaffer, a consistent winner of teacher of the year awards from Portland, Oregon, whose students have made incredible strides in the past decade, winning ten Oregon Stock Market Games in a row. This semiannual competition is sponsored by Portland State University and the Oregon Council of Economic Education. I listened to Schaffer, this track coach and teacher of the year, speak about topics that most people never fully understand.

It was at this time that I realized the power of the material I was learning, and I began to understand that others also wanted to understand these concepts. Most people had questions, but they were unsure of

---

9   Abraham, Jay, *Getting Everything You Can Out of All that You've Got* (New York: St. Martin's Press, 2000).
10   Gove, Bill, *The Ultimate Speaking Package*, DVD (Boynton Beach, Florida: Gove-Siebold).

where to turn to learn the answers. I decided to search for these answers. I then formed a mastermind group which undertook the task of answering these questions in a book that aimed to explain The Laws of the Universe—*Living in Harmony by Natural Law*.[11] These days, The Law of Attraction is very commonly known, and it is used in many books. But in 2001, when Friends of the Renaissance, of which I am a member, wrote the book, very few people knew what we were talking about. There was a great need to explain this material to the masses in a way that could be easily understood. I am still in contact with this author group, and we are currently discussing publishing a second edition of this book.

After moving to Phoenix, Arizona, in early 2001, I met more people who were studying this material. The area is home to many spiritual thinkers who write books that they hope will help people understand themselves. *The Power of Now: A Guide to Spiritual Enlightenment* explains the "pain body"[12] that holds us back, and *Power vs. Force*[13] shows us how we can reach higher levels of enlightenment by changing our thoughts, feelings, and moods, thus raising our levels of vibration.

It was at this point in time that I started to put the material into practice. This is a very important point to make. Anyone can quote knowledge, but the key is to translate the knowledge you have learned into results. The only way one can tell if they really understand these ideas would be if they chose to take a close and honest look at their results. If the results are good, the person is likely on the right track. That person may simply need some fine tuning to take their results to a higher level. If the results are not good, it might be time for the person to get back to the drawing board and take a good look at the way they think. If a person is unhappy with any aspect of his life, time, effort, and persistence can change things.

11   Friends of the Renaissance, *Living in Harmony by Natural Law* (Salt Lake City: Envision Press, 2001).
12   Tolle, Eckhart. *The Power of Now: A Guide to Spiritual Enlightenment.* Vancouver, Canada, Namaste Publishing, 1999.
13   Hawkins, David R., *Power vs. Force: The Hidden Determinants of Human Behavior* (Sedona, AZ: Veritas Publishing, 1995).

I was unhappy with the results of my life in 2001. At the time, it seemed that life just wasn't going the way I had planned. The September 11, 2001, terrorist attacks knocked many people off course. As a result, many businesses had to divert to a new course of direction. It was then that I realized that in order to do the things I wanted to do, I had to start to live my life according to the material I had learned. This is when I began to implement the ideas I'd learned in the previous years. This implementation of ideas required a serious shift in the way I thought about things. It was difficult to move forward when I didn't know anything about the place I was headed. I simply had to trust myself and the people I had studied with. With this trust on my side, I made calculated moves in an effort to realize my dreams. It was at this time that I wrote *The Secret for Teens Revealed*. As I wrote, I used the material as a mentoring tool to guide many young people.

At the height of my uncertainty, in 2002, I attended a seminar given by Dr. Joseph Guan. At this seminar, I learned about Emotional Freedom Technique (EFT). This technique would help me eliminate phobias, abandon self-limiting beliefs, and strengthen my self-esteem. These techniques improved my life by allowing me to focus on the positive side of all situations and by helping me to work through negative situations that can hold me back. This seminar was incredible. Not only did Guan become a close friend and mentor, but he also helped me learn, understand, and perfect the EFT procedure so I could implement it on my own. This seminar, along with the knowledge I learned from Proctor, allowed me to take the concepts I had learned and actually put them into practice. This truly is the missing link that most people do not recognize. There is no use attending seminars and reading books if you are not willing or able to put the knowledge you learn into action.

When the movie *The Secret* was released in 2006, it helped others to understand what I had been trying to convey. This movie, and another titled *What the Bleep Do We Know!?*, have tremendously helped the material to become mainstream and understood by the masses. Since *The Secret* was such a blockbuster hit, I decided that it was the best time for me to release my ideas to help parents and teachers gain a sound understanding of their own thinking. My goal is to then have these adults teach these principles to their teenagers and students. It is also my hope that teens will have a chance to contemplate their own ways of thinking and consider how slight modifications could make a significant impact on their lives.

Greg Link, cofounder and president of CoveyLink Worldwide, noted that "97% of adults have not learned these secrets and even less live by them." He suggests that teens empower themselves to "master your mind and rule your world—and your parents."[14] This is a powerful concept to imagine. Most adults who begin to study these concepts marvel at how much faster they could have achieved their goals if only they had learned these ideas when they were younger.

To this day, I remain a student of this material. Currently, I am enjoying learning more about the unseen world by reading Sylvia Browne's books. Also, Wayne Dyer's book, *There's a Spiritual Solution to Every Problem*,[15] has given me much insight into balancing my life. I continue to challenge myself by attending speeches given by world-class speakers at the weeklong *Principia* seminar held annually by PSI Seminars in Clearlake Oaks, California. This seminar company was instrumental in my discovery of strategies for life success.

Another set of tools that have helped me gain a deeper understanding of this material comes from the Abraham-Hicks monthly CD subscription program, through which I receive an audio CD once a month that is recorded directly from Abraham Hicks's live seminars. This connection allows me to continue to think positively while helping me to think of new ways to move toward my goals. Each CD features a lesson and then questions and answers from other people, just like me, who are also trying to realize their goals. Whenever I feel myself straying off course, I plug in a CD while I am driving to work, and I am amazed at how quickly I can turn my thinking around with a little help. As often as I can, I work on staying positive because I know this is the only way to move toward my goals.

14   Link, Greg Co-Founder and President of CoveyLink Worldwide (May 2008)
15   Dyer, Wayne *There is a Spiritual Solution to Every Problem* (New York: Harper Collins, 2003).

I am still searching for answers to my questions. And as time goes on, I find more and more information that helps me gain a deeper understanding of my purpose in life, which feels exciting and full of adventure. Each day, I uncover something new, something that I had never before seen in this world. Have you ever reread a book and learned things that you missed the first time? The book has not changed; you have. Eventually, you will notice that the world around you is constantly changing. Therefore, so are you.

I wish you the best as you pursue your studies, and I know that you will experience many positive life changes once these ideas are implemented. Get ready for an adventure!

Best of luck, and have fun.

History and Testimonials

Take a look at the history of this program, and you will see where the ideas first originated. You will also be exposed to some actual results via testimonials from youth who have studied this material as well as programs of similar nature.

Youth Mentor International

Bob Proctor launched the YMI program in January 1999. In doing so, he accepted a challenge from some colleagues who wanted to see if he could teach to children the concepts he was already so successful at teaching to members of the business world. Twelve youth began the program by studying concepts similar to those presented in *The Secret for Teens Revealed*. Within a few months, the program's membership skyrocketed to more than five hundred youth.

Easter Seals' Leaders of Tomorrow Program

Andrea Samadi wrote her own curriculum that mirrors the activities in *The Secret for Teens Revealed* and mentored one hundred youth from the Easter Seals Society from July 2002 to 2005. Each participating youth had a physical disability. The results were astounding, and they mirrored that of Proctor's YMI Program. Andrea Samadi won the Helping Hands award in October 2005 for using these concepts with Easter Seals.

Secret for Teens Revealed

In 2008, Andrea Samadi releases *The Secret for Teens Revealed*. She holds a vision of helping parents, teachers and teenagers build a solid foundation for a purpose-filled life.

Next, you will hear from some of the youth who went through this program; you will see how their lives have forever changed by studying these secret concepts. Also, hear from some adults who have been using these concepts, and wish that they had learned them sooner.

Testimonials

Justin Artale of Windsor, Ontario, Canada

The Leaders of Tomorrow program has taught me the importance of setting goals. If you plan your work and work your plan, great things can be accomplished. As a result of the values and skills that I have gained through my involvement in the program, I am able to better advocate both for myself and for all persons with disabilities. By bringing to light our plight, I am helping to raise public awareness, which will assist in the development of solutions while encouraging individuals with disabilities to achieve their full potential.

Naeem Baccus of Newmarket, Ontario, Canada

The Leaders of Tomorrow is a fantastic program that gave me the skills to work towards success with my personal and academic goals. Through consultation with my mentoring coach, Andrea Samadi, I could openly discuss my difficulties and discover useful tips from her and my fellow peers with disabilities. I was then able to look at new situations, or ones I had been through, from a different perspective. I learned that by thinking positively and developing simple strategies, I could overcome many of life's everyday challenges.

The benefit of working with the Leaders of Tomorrow program through Easter Seals is that it empowers teens and young adults to focus and achieve their personal goals. The coach listens and provides feedback, thereby facilitating open discussion among all participants. This program is unique because it allows those with disabilities the opportunity to share their experiences with others.

The program allowed me to improve my life, by enhancing my friendships, manage my stress levels, and balancing my time. It showed me how positive thinking could help me to develop self confidence. Being part of the Leaders of Tomorrow program has enabled me to be a role model for other youth, whether or not they are disabled.

I feel privileged to have been involved in this program, and it has given me a great sense of achievement. I would definitely recommend it to others.

Mike Brooks, Mr. Inside Sales, Author, Consultant, Trainer of Woodland Hills, California

After reading through Andrea's book, The Secrets for Teens Revealed, all I could think of was, "Why didn't this book come out when I was a teen?!" Everything I wished I had learned as a teenager—the importance of goal setting, developing healthy self-esteem, living in alignment with my values—I finally did learn through years of trial and error, but if I had Andrea's wonderful book back then, there's no telling how far I'd have risen—and how much quicker!

The Secrets for Teens Revealed should be required reading or teens and their parents (as well as teachers, administrators, etc.), and for anyone else who still wants to make the most of their life and life experience.

A GEM of a book!

Theresa Tindall, Art Director, Toronto, Ontario

I would lay in my room and imagine the kind of people I wanted to know … as I felt I didn't know any at that time … supportive, open to knowing me instead of projecting onto me, etc. I imagined living in a beautiful place with my friends and doing lots of adventurous things and being very excited about my life … exposure to culture, beauty and nature. None of these things were happening at the time.

Then one morning I woke up and I was only a year or so older. I was now living in California in a beautiful house that three very incredible friends and I shared. I was now a scuba diver had travelled … became friends with so many wonderful people. These three women are still my good friends … twenty five years later and we travel many miles to see each other every year … all from lying down peacefully in my room and feeling the feelings I wanted to have when before I knew it, all these things finally happened. It was amazing. My life has had many exciting adventures ever since.

Now It's Your Turn to Study

Dear parents, teachers, and *The Secret for Teens Revealed* students,

Do you realize how lucky you are to have access to this knowledge? I will say loud and clear throughout this program that with The Secret Revealed, you will be expected to implement these ideas into your daily life.

Parents and teachers will be given specific instructions that detail how each lesson will assist them. Teenagers will also be given instructions detailing what they should be thinking about to attain the desired results from each lesson. I know that together, we will see many positive changes just from making a few simple changes in the coming year of study. I am sure you picked up this book either because you've already experienced incredible results from studying The Secret or you are curious about ways that you can accelerate your journey to your goals. It would be no surprise to me if you wanted to learn more, help others understand this material, and take your understanding to the next level. That is exactly why this guide was written.

As you read in the preface, I began to study this personal development material in 1997 after meeting Bob Proctor, a man who has been studying these concepts for more than forty years. He took some of these ideas to Fortune 500 companies and helped them attain significant results. Then, Reid Nelson and Al Keranen, Proctor's colleagues, challenged Proctor to take these concepts to teenagers. He began his Youth Mentor International Program in January 1999. The results the teens experienced were so profound that I decided to resign as a schoolteacher to work with Proctor. I wanted to learn some of his theories so that one day I would be able take them back into the classrooms and introduce them to the home lives of young people around the world. As the former executive director of YMI and salesperson for a seminar titled The Science of Getting Rich, I saw teens go from earning failing grades to earning As, from warming the bench to starting games, and from having no confidence to having unlimited confidence. It was truly amazing.

In 2002, I rewrote the curriculum for youth and called it the Mentoring Excellence Now 2002 program. One hundred youth from the Easter Seals Society in Toronto, Canada, were introduced to these concepts as a part of the Leaders of Tomorrow Program. These youth achieved significant results, just like with the youth involved in Proctor's YMI Program. The Easter Seals Society presented me with The Helping Hand Award in October 2005 the success that these youth had attained.

It was also quite a learning experience for me as a teacher of the material. I learned the concepts more deeply as I explained them and then was amazed at how fast the youth picked up the ideas that had taken me much longer to comprehend. Now, I am talking about youth with physical disabilities here, but they would not let their disabilities affect their goals or become excuses for their results. I would end the teaching sessions so amazed at the power that the students possessed that I was often prevented from making excuses about my own growth.

In April 2006, the movie *The Secret* shook the foundations of the world. People everywhere began speaking of the concepts Proctor had been teaching for most of his life. It was at this time that I knew I had to put *The Secret for Teens Revealed* into print. Many youth have gained tremendous results by studying, understanding, and then implementing these truths into their lives.

Byrne reminds of us this fact in the very beginning of *The Secret*. It was her daughter, Hailey, who handed Byrne the book *The Science of Getting Rich*, by Wallace D Wattles,[1] who urged her mother to create the most talked-about movie and book in the personal development industry. I look forward to hearing how your life has been enhanced by studying and understanding this material.

Congratulations to parents, teachers, and teens who have taken these initial steps toward personal development. I know firsthand that the concepts in the text to follow will change your life if you are able to understand them and implement them. I strongly believe that the knowledge you will gain will be more powerful, and the information you gather will be more helpful, than that which most people learn at an institution of higher learning. Your life will never be the same.

I look forward to sharing this adventure with you.

Sincere and fond appreciation,
Andrea Samadi

---

1   Wattles, Wallace D., *The Science of Getting Rich* (Tarcher, 2007).

Foreword

Here is a message to you from Bob Proctor, a teacher from the movie The Secret.

 Hello, and welcome to *The Secret for Teens Revealed* study guide and workbook. I want to let you, the reader, know that I have been studying this material for more than forty years and have helped thousands of people to build lives of prosperity, self-discovery, goal achievement, and success. I believe that every person has unlimited potential within them, and unlocking this potential and putting the material to proper use is the key to turning one's dreams into reality. This does include you.

I know this is the key because in the 1960s, I was a high school dropout with a bleak outlook for the future. This was true until I picked up the book *Think and Grow Rich* by Napoleon Hill and began to look at life in a different way.

After I began to study these concepts and had some mentors who saw more in me than I could see in myself, something started to click for me. My life completely turned around, and I started to experience incredible success.

I decided to spend some time trying to understand what I had done to achieve this success. I was confused because many of my friends took my advice, but none of them experienced the results I'd attained. They did not understand The Laws of Success that are explained in this program.

I am going to suggest that you take these ideas very seriously, and you will be amazed at the many turns your life will take. You will begin to understand life-changing concepts that most people have never been taught. Imagine what can happen when your whole family gets involved with these ideas and uses these new concepts as well. Imagine how great you will feel when you can teach others what you have mastered. The results you see in both your personal and professional life will soar.

I have helped thousands of adults worldwide to see dramatic changes with their results, and I have watched teens go from being C-students to being A-students. They've gone from sitting on the bench to playing in the starting lineup. And they've developed stronger relationships with teachers, parents, and siblings by merely changing a few things about the way they think and the things they do. Imagine how your life will change when you start to implement these ideas yourself.

Welcome to the most powerful material you will ever study. I wish you an exciting life of prosperity and success.

Sincerely,

Introduction and Purpose
Behind This Study Guide

The purpose of this guide is to assist teachers and parents as they teach the concepts Proctor teaches so successfully to adults in his seminars. For more than forty years, Proctor has helped people become more aware as they seek exciting lives and pursue their dreams, and I wanted to share these ideas with you.

I also wanted to create a guide for teenagers to help them find the right path or direction in their lives. I know how difficult high school can be, and I know that having a strong sense of your values and self-esteem will help you to get through these uncertain years. Once you look back, you will see that the cornerstone to your success really started at this crucial time. The self-esteem that you develop while you are young will carry you through the challenging times you will inevitably face in your future.

How to Use
This Study Guide

Each of the ten lessons contains a five-step approach to learning.

1. **Prepare:** Here, you will be asked to complete a preassessment of the topic to be taught to prepare yourself for the lesson. You will be asked some questions that will help you learn and understand the lesson better.

    •   Parents and teachers, imagine if you could take these ideas and put them to work on your teenagers or students. They could learn all the treasures found in the movie *The Secret*. Or maybe you are looking for answers yourself. The activities in this guide will help you gain some understanding of yourself, and once you begin to understand these concepts, you can share them with others. If you are a parent, you might want your family to understand these concepts so there will be a common ground of understanding in your home. If you are a teacher, these would be great topics to cover in class.

    •   Teenagers and young adults, maybe you have been looking for some direction in your life. From time to time, most of us question whether we are headed in the right direction. This happens even if we are in the middle of our careers. Having a solid understanding of who you are will keep you on track with your life goals.

2. **Think About This!** This section will address parents and teachers with some things to think about as they move through the lesson. Teenagers will also be addressed with some concepts to reflect on.

3. **Lesson:** This is where you will be taught the top-secret concepts to help you build a successful life and future.

4. **Review:** You will be asked to check your understanding and comprehension of the lesson here.

5. **Extension Exercises**: This section will help you to apply the concepts to your everyday life to achieve proven and predictable results.

Implementation Ideas for School Administration and Teachers

If you already have a character education program implemented within your school, you can use *The Secret for Teens Revealed* to supplement the program you already have working for you. Erik Khilji, principal with the York Region District School Board, in Toronto, Canada, notes that "Character education should be taught in the classrooms and integrated into every subject." Khilji believes that educators play an important role with raising student achievement.

For example, he notes that

> [W]e have recognition assemblies every month … each month we choose one character trait (for example responsibility this month), and each teacher chooses two students who best exemplify this trait that month. At the assembly, the student is recognized with a certificate in front of the school, and their parents are invited to the assembly. Another example is Random Acts of Kindness. Every morning, I read out on the morning announcements random acts of kindness demonstrated by students that teachers submit to me.

> When the students feel that teachers want them to succeed, then they will perform to the best of their abilities. They need to know that their teachers are behind them and want them to reach high levels of achievement. This means raising the bar so that the students will work to meet the expectations

and equity of outcomes is a priority. Parents must be engaged and work together with the school. When their children see this happening, they will work harder and smarter. And there should be co-curricular activities for all students. This creates a healthy environment, and students can benefit from these experiences that will help them later in life. And teachers can develop better relationships with students outside of the classroom which will transfer into the classroom which will result in improved student achievement.[1]

Khilji recites a story that he's proud of because it changed one of his students' life:

At one of my schools, I became aware of a student who had a reputation of being behaviorally challenged. One day when I spoke with him in my office he told me that he didn't understand the work in classes. When I looked into it, it turned out that Jerome, a grade 8 student, who failed the year before, was working at a grade 2 level in literacy. No wonder he was having difficulty. He was trying to be the cool guy so no one could find out that he can't read, and at the same time his self-esteem was diminishing. We got him support, had him assessed, so that he can achieve success. Later, he told me I was a good principal because I listened to him. If I hadn't listened to him and taken immediate action, he may have been just another unsuccessful pathway's statistic who wouldn't graduate from high school. Today he is grade 9, still receiving support, but he can read. Sometimes I drive by the high school that he attends on the way home, and I see him running on the track. That's better than running the streets, which may have happened. It's important that as educators we take the time to listen. This is an example that as a principal, I have more opportunity to listen to and to communicate my expectation that every child can learn, and will learn.

---

1   Khilji, Erik, principal, York Region District School Board, Toronto, Canada, 2008.

Jim Carson, principal at Burrows Hall Public School, Toronto, Ontario, agrees with the importance of character education being taught and supported at the school level. He noted that "The Toronto District School Board held a survey in which students, staff, and parents had an opportunity to vote to select the character traits they feel should be the focus of character education in the TDSB. They selected: kindness and caring, cooperation, fairness, honesty, integrity, perseverance, respect, responsibility, empathy, and teamwork." Carson added that "resources will be provided for teachers, but these character-building concepts need to be supported by schoolwide initiatives to model, support, and celebrate them. They will need to be infused into the curriculum."[2]

I have also seen the Character Counts Curriculum used successfully in many schools in the United States that focus on the "Six Pillars of Character: trustworthiness, respect, responsibility, fairness, caring, and citizenship."[3] These six core ethical values form the core of the Josephson Institute's programs that have helped over 5 million kids in 51 countries with these Six Pillars of Character that bolster student achievement and self-esteem.

Plan for Parents, Teachers, and Teens

The Secret for Teens Revealed promotes excellence on a daily basis. As a student of personal development, you are a role model to everyone around you. It is recommended that you read and complete the activities in this program and follow the directions that are provided. There is no use in picking up this book if you are not seriously committed to completing the activities. If you want to be a winner in life, then read on.

This guide begins with your participation. Once you start to study this material, you will not want to stop. As you see life-changing results within yourself, you will no doubt become a lifetime student of personal development and self-improvement. Maybe you have already begun to study. Maybe you have already experienced some

---

2 Carson, Jim, principal at Burrows Hall Public School, Toronto, Ontario.

3 CharacterCounts.org

remarkable results. Now is the time to use the assessment at the beginning of the guide to pinpoint areas of your life that you would like to improve.

You will begin by taking a closer look at your different learning styles. You'll do this by completing the Multiple Intelligence Activity. Next, you will learn how you think and which side of your brain you rely on most. You will also learn to understand your many different learning styles. This will be very powerful. You will learn your strengths so you can in turn manage your weaknesses.

You will be taught and reminded of ten top-secret concepts in this study guide. There will be a preassessment before each lesson and questions throughout the material that will check your comprehension as you progress through the program. This format is in place to help you gauge how familiar with the concepts you are before you delve into a new topic. This format also allows you to track your improvements as you move forward. Parents and teachers will be asked to think about how they would like to implement the ten concepts for a better quality of life, and teenagers will be asked to reflect on how they will use this program to work toward a life they thought was only possible in their dreams.

Outcomes of the Program: Once you have completed *The Secret for Teens Revealed* study guide and workbook, you will have a stronger understanding of your life's purpose and your passions. You will have a sense of who you are, and it will become easy for you to model the exercises for others. You will become excited about your own life, so much so that when you are speaking with others about these concepts, you will become equally excited to know that they will soon be enlightened. You will also be better able to assist them with their own self-discovery.

***The Secret for Teens Revealed* focuses on the way your thoughts control your personal achievement.** *Everyone must understand that each person determines his or her own destiny, and we only have one shot at this thing called life. There are no second chances. If you mess it up, you have only yourself to blame.* I will remind you again that successful implementation of the ideas within *The Secret for Teens Revealed* requires that you actually incorporate the material into your daily life. If you don't, the material will simply remain as theories in your mind as opposed to realities in your life.

The most effective way to work through *The Secret for Teens Revealed* is to learn, understand, and then implement the ideas. This implementation is the missing link that most people do not understand. They intellectually understand the concepts, but knowing and doing are miles apart.

This year, it will be important for you to think about the results you would like to attain. Think of this program as a benchmark for progress or a turning point in your life. You will learn ideas that are capable of taking you to new heights and changing your life. As important as focusing outwardly on your work, school, friends, and family are, it is equally important that you focus inward on the action you plan to take in regard to your mental/spiritual attitude. What good would it do to put all your efforts into your job or your schoolwork while simultaneously neglecting friendships and relationships? On the other hand, you also need to think about how much you will contribute to society by giving back some of your time and efforts to others. It is important to stay in balance as you strive for excellence. You will also need to learn to hold this balance after you reach your end result.

Keep in mind that the information you will learn is not new. The philosopher Francis Bacon studied these concepts back in the 1600s. These concepts have been around for centuries but are not practiced by many people. This guide will give you a direct link to this powerful knowledge. In turn, you will be able to share the ideas with others or simply learn to perfect them in your own life. Imagine how powerful it will be to see your family members move in the direction of their dreams and toward a successful life of liberty, joy, peace, and harmony.

I suggest that you mentally prepare yourself for this year of study. You are being given an opportunity that most people are never afforded. It is the opportunity to study yourself and your mind. Enjoy, and I hope that you continue to explore your mind for many years to come.

COMMITMENT STATEMENT

I commit to studying this material. I will focus on reading each chapter, answering all questions honestly, and taking a close look at the results I am producing. If I do not like the results I see, I will not blame anyone else. I will take full responsibility for my future, and I will take charge of the impact I plan to have on the world around me. Once I have a sound understanding of the concepts, I plan to expose others to them. I will also work with others so they can achieve their own understanding.

Signature:_____

Date: _____

Name of Commitment Partner: _____

Personal Inventory for Parents, Teachers, and Teenagers

Answer these questions as honestly as possible. This exercise will help you pinpoint the areas of your life that need the most focus.

Work Life/Academics

1. How are your relationships with your coworkers or with friends at school? Explain.

_____

_____

_____

2. Would you like to improve your relationships with your coworkers or friends? If yes, why?

_____

_____

_____

_____

3. Are you able to communicate openly and effectively with all your coworkers or friends? Give examples.

_____

_____

_____

_____

4. If not, what gets in the way from clear communication?

_____

_____

_____

_____

5. What steps are you willing to take to improve your relationships with your coworkers?

_____

_____

_____

_____

_____

Peers

1. What do you and your peers do in your spare time?

_____

_____

_____

_____

2. Do you get along well with your friends? If not, why?

_____

_____

_____

_____

3. If you have spats with your friends, do you deal with them? If yes, how?

_____

_____

_____

_____

4. What steps are you willing to take to improve your relationship with your peers?

_____

_____

_____

_____

_____

_____

Social Activities

1. What do you like to do when you are not at work or school?

   _____

   _____

   _____

   _____

2. Do you think you use your spare time productively, or do you think you waste time? Explain honestly.

   _____

   _____

   _____

   _____

   _____

3. How much time do you spend watching television?

   _____

4. Are you willing to give up some of your free time to do something productive (i.e. volunteer)? If you were to volunteer or do something productive, what would you like to do?

   _____

   _____

   _____

   _____

   _____

Family Life

1. How openly and freely can you discuss any topic with other members of your family?

   _____

   _____

   _____

   _____

   _____

2. Do you and your family members have mutual respect for each other? If not, explain why you think someone is being disrespectful.

_____

_____

_____

_____

_____

3. What steps are you willing to take to make sure respect is always present when family members are concerned?

_____

_____

_____

_____

_____

4. Do you discuss the major aspects of your life and how you feel about life with your family members?

_____

_____

_____

5. If not, what would it take to be able to share your life with the members of your family?

_____

_____

_____

_____

_____

_____

6. Do you always have respect for your siblings?

_____

_____

_____

_____

7. What steps are you willing to take to ensure that respect is always present?

    _____

    _____

    _____

    _____

8. How do you handle upsets or disagreements with your siblings?

    _____

    _____

    _____

    _____

9. Do you get along with all your relatives?

    _____

    _____

    _____

    _____

Other family issues

1. Are there any other family issues you feel need to be discussed?

    _____

    _____

    _____

    _____

2. How do you feel about the love, support, and attention you are getting in your life?

    _____

    _____

    _____

    _____

    _____

3. Do you give back to others love, support, and attention?

_____

_____

_____

_____

Physical Activity

1. What physical activities do you enjoy? Explain.

_____

_____

_____

_____

_____

_____

_____

_____

2. Are you getting enough exercise?

_____

_____

_____

_____

3. What steps are you willing to take to ensure you are getting enough exercise?

_____

_____

_____

_____

Music and the Arts

1. Do you enjoy music and the arts?

_____

_____

_____

_____

2. What do you enjoy about them?

_____

_____

_____

_____

3. If you do not enjoy music and the arts, are you willing to investigate them further?

_____

_____

Your Strengths

1. What are you really good at?

_____

_____

_____

_____

2. What things do you really like to do?

_____

_____

_____

_____

3. If you could choose a future job, one that you really love, what would it be?

_____

_____

_____

_____

4. What are you willing to do to kick your strengths up a notch and improve upon what you are already good at?

_____

_____

_____

_____

Your Future

1. What is your current vision for your future? Let your mind soar.

_____

_____

_____

_____

_____

_____

_____

2. If you had a choice, what would you love to spend all day doing?

_____

_____

_____

_____

_____

_____

_____

Important Qualities

1. Who do you admire? List two people. They can be famous people or people you know.

_____

_____

2. What qualities do you admire in those people?

_____

_____

_____

_____

_____

_____

3. Do you feel you have these qualities?

_____

_____

_____

_____

4. If yes, how could you improve upon them?

_____

_____

_____

_____

_____

_____

5. If no, what are you willing to do to develop these qualities?

_____

_____

_____

_____

_____

_____

Personal Inventory

1. Name things that are part of your life though you wish they were not present.

_____

_____

_____

_____

_____

2. How often do you think about these things?

_____

_____

3. Do you realize that the things we focus on the most are the things we attract into our lives? Explain.

_____

_____

_____

_____

PART ONE

Understanding Your Learning Styles

For success in class, exploring your learning style is essential.[1]

Howard Gardner

---

1   Gardner, Howard, *Frames of Mind* (New York: Basic Books, 1983).

Think
About This!

- For parents and teachers, this section will help you understand and recognize your learning styles. In turn, you will be able teach your children and students with more insight.

- For teenagers, this section will help you understand which learning styles and intelligences are your strongest. It will also guide you toward learning which areas are less developed. This understanding will help you further strengthen areas of weakness or continue to solidify your areas of strength.

Lesson

Professor Howard Gardner developed the Multiple Intelligence Theory. It was his belief that there are at least eight different intelligences possessed by all people, and that some intelligences are more highly developed than others. Have you ever learned something very quickly and easily? You were probably using one of your more developed intelligences. On the other hand, have you ever struggled with a topic, and no matter how hard you tried, it seemed impossible to grasp? You were most likely wrestling with one of your underdeveloped intelligences. To discover your most developed and under developed intelligences, take this test. It will put you at ease with your new understanding. Finally, you can take your new knowledge to the next level and actually choose courses in school that support your strengths. In this regard, so you can gear the direction of your studies to best suit the career of your choice. If need be, you can obtain the assistance necessary to strengthen a weak area early on in your academic career rather than waiting until after graduation to wonder what action you could or should have taken earlier.

Learning Styles and
Multiple Intelligences

Research from Howard Gardner's Frames of Mind

Learning is a complex process that involves taking in information, interpreting that information, and associating it with information you already know. With so much involved in learning, it would make sense that styles of learning vary widely from person to person. A group of people can hear the same information yet respond with different notes, interpretation, perception, and levels of retention.

The more you know about how you take in information, the more you will be able to adjust to the different teaching styles of different teachers. Your mind is the most powerful tool you will ever possess. You are capable of developing many skills and you can process all kinds of information. However, when you have trouble accomplishing a particular task, you may become convinced that you cannot learn how to do anything new. You may feel that those who can do what you cannot do are better equipped to learn than you are. Not only is this perception incorrect, but it can also damage your self-esteem.

Every individual is highly developed in some areas and lacking in other areas. Many successful people are brilliant in one area and function poorly in another.

Slow starters can be strong finishers.

Did you know:

- Winston Churchill failed sixth grade. Sir Winston Churchill (1874–1965) was a British politician known mainly for his leadership of Great Britain during World War II.

- Abraham Lincoln was demoted to the rank of private during the Black Hawk War. Abe Lincoln (1809–1865) was the sixteenth President of the United States.

- Louis Pasteur was a poor student in chemistry. Louis Pasteur (1822–1895), a French chemist and microbiologist, is best known for remarkable breakthroughs in disease prevention.

- Albert Einstein could not speak until he was four years old, and he did not read until he was seven. His parents and teachers worried about his mental ability. Albert Einstein (1879–1955) was a German-born physicist who was best known for his Theory of Relativity and mass–energy equivalence ($E = mc^2$). He received the Nobel Prize in physics in 1921.

- Ludwig van Beethoven's music teacher said of Beethoven, "As a composer, he is hopeless."[1] Beethoven (1770–1827), a German composer and pianist, remains one of the most respected and influential composers of all time.

- When Thomas Edison was a young boy, his teachers said he was so stupid he could never learn anything. He once said, "I remember, I used to never be able to get along at school. I was always at the foot of my class … my father thought I was stupid, and I almost decided that I was a dunce."[2] Thomas Edison (1847–1931) was an American inventor who is most commonly known for inventing the phonograph and the lightbulb.

- When F. W. Woolworth was twenty-one, he got a job in a store, but he was not allowed to wait on customers because he "didn't have enough sense."[3] F. W. Woolworth (1852–1919) founded the retail store Woolworth's in 1878 with a loan of three hundred dollars.

1   Thompson, Michael *Our Gifted Children* Magazine, Unionville, NY, March 2001
2   Thompson, ibid
3   Thompson, ibid

When sculptor Auguste Rodin was young, he had difficulty learning to read and write. Today, we might say he had a learning disability, but his father said of him, "I have an idiot for a son." His uncle agreed. "He's uneducable,"[4] the uncle said. Rodin (1840–1917) is most famous for being a sculptor.

- A newspaper editor once fired Walt Disney because he thought Disney had no good ideas. Walt Disney (1901–1966) became one of the most well-known motion picture producers in the world.

- Enrico Caruso was told by a music teacher, "You can't sing. You have no voice at all." Caruso (1873–1921) is remembered as one of the greatest Italian tenor opera singers in history.

- An editor told Louisa May Alcott that she was incapable of writing anything that would have popular appeal. Alcott (1832–1888), an American novelist, wrote the novel *Little Women* in 1868.

What if these people had listened to the negative things said about their undeveloped learning styles and become discouraged? Where would our world be without the music of Beethoven, the art of Rodin, or the ideas of Albert Einstein and Thomas Edison? Remember, just because you may be underdeveloped in one area does not mean all of your intelligences are this way. We have multiple intelligences, and it is up to you to discover which ones you have developed more than others. Then, you can use your strengths to move you ahead at a rapid clip.

> It's not what you are; it's what you don't become that hurts.
> *Oscar Levant (1906–1874), an American*
> *pianist, composer, author, comedian, and actor.*

Life is truly what we make of it. I know we all have tremendous amounts of power within us that can bring forth serious results. This happens when we use our talents to the best of our ability.

---

4 Thompson, ibid

It is of the utmost importance that we recognize and nurture all of the varied human intelligences and all of the combinations of intelligences. ... If we can mobilize the spectrum of human abilities, not only will people feel better about themselves and more competent, it is even possible that they will also feel more engaged and better able to join the rest of the community in working for the broader good. Perhaps, if you can mobilize the full range of human intelligences and ally them to an ethical sense, we can help to increase the likelihood of our survival on this planet and perhaps even contribute to our thriving.

Howard Gardner

Multiple
Intelligences Test

Take this test to see how you learn best.

Directions

Using the scale below, rate each of the provided statements. Write the number of the ranking on the line next to the statement. Then, add the numbers for each section to learn your total score for that particular intelligence. Next, log your scores on the scoring chart which follows the questions. You will be able to see which of your intelligences are highly developed, which are moderately developed, and which are underdeveloped based on the numbers you score. You can read about specific intelligences once you complete this exercise. Finally, complete the follow-up activities to further expose your learning strength and weakness.

Rate each statement as follows:
1 = hardly ever
2 = some of the time
3 = usually
4 = always

1. _____   I enjoy exercising.

2. _____   I do not enjoy sitting still.

3. _____   I prefer to learn through activities.

4. _____   I move my legs or hands when I am told to sit still.

5. _____   I enjoy working with my hands to create new things.

6. _____ I like to pace around the room when I am thinking or studying.

_____ **Total for Bodily-Kinesthetic**

7. _____ I am good at navigating with a map and don't need a GPS system.

8. _____ I like to draw pictures or diagrams when explaining ideas to others.

9. _____ I can assemble items easily from diagrams by following directions.

10._____ I enjoy drawing or photography.

11._____ I like reading novels.

12._____ I prefer to look at a drawn map over following written directions.

_____ **Total for Visual-Spatial**

13._____ I enjoy telling stories.

14._____ I like to write stories.

15._____ I enjoy reading for long periods of time.

16._____ I express myself clearly with words.

17._____ I am good at negotiating to get what I want.

18._____ I like to discuss and debate topics that interest me.

_____ **Total for Verbal-Linguistic**

19. _____ I like math and working with numbers.

20._____ I like science and enjoy learning new things about the world.

21._____ I am good at problem solving.

22._____ I question how things work to make improvements.

23._____ I enjoy planning or designing something new that will be more efficient.

24._____ I am good at fixing things and am a forward thinker.

_____ **Total for Logical-Mathematical**

25._____ I enjoy listening to music and have many different playlists on my iPod.

26._____ I cannot help dancing when I hear music.

27._____ I have a good sense of rhythm.

28._____ I like to sing along with music.

29._____ People have told me that I am talented musically.

30._____ Music I hear helps me create new ideas.

_____ **Total for Musical**

31._____ I like doing group projects.

32._____ People come to me to help settle conflicts.

33._____ I like to spend time with other people. (Friends and family)

34._____ I am good at understanding people and have ideas to solve problems.

35._____ I am good at making people feel comfortable in most situations.

36._____   I enjoy helping others when asked.

_____   **Total for Interpersonal**

37._____   I need quiet time to think, read, and reflect on my life.

38._____   I think deeply about issues before I want to talk about them.

39._____   I am interested in self-improvement, the mind, and human potential.

40._____   I understand and am able to control my thoughts, feelings, and results.

41._____   I am currently working on at least five goals.

42._____   I prefer to work on projects alone.

_____   **Total for Intrapersonal**

43._____   I enjoy being outside whenever possible.

44._____   I fantasize about having a career involving nature or the outdoors.

45._____   I enjoy studying plants, animals, or oceans.

46._____   I avoid being inside my house except when I sleep.

47._____   When I was younger, I played with spiders, small bugs, and liked fishing.

48._____   When I am stressed, I feel better if I go for a walk or hike outside.

_____   **Total for Naturalistic**

Below, write each intelligence on the chart according to your score.

Take a look at your scores to see which intelligences you have that are highly developed and which are less developed.

20-24 Highly Developed	14-19 Moderately Developed	0-14 Less Developed

Debriefing each intelligence

Bodily/Kinesthetic Intelligence

These learners have the ability to move their bodies with ease and skill. They have a good sense of balance, coordination, and endurance.

Possible career interests: Athlete, physical education teacher, dancer, actor, firefighter.

Suggested action steps to further develop these skills:

- Take a new exercise class—tae kwon do, Pilates, kick boxing, or yoga.

- Consult a personal trainer about your current exercise routine to get tips for improvement.

- Practice visualization to increase your muscle memory. It is proven that if athletes think through their workouts, their brains will actually think their bodies are performing the actions. To perfect your moves, think about them before you go to sleep at night.

Your thoughts: Who do you know who is strong in the area of Bodily/Kinesthetic Intelligence? Explain.

_____

_____

_____

_____

_____

_____

Visual/Spatial Intelligence

Visual learners tend to think in pictures and need to create vivid mental images to retain information. They enjoy navigating with maps, using charts, taking or studying photographs, and watching videos and movies.

Possible career interests: Interior designer, architect, building engineer, artist.

These people are suited for any job that involves designing or creating something visual.

Suggested action steps to further develop these skills:

- Purchase a model airplane kit and practice putting it together.

- Put together puzzles.

- Help someone design their backyard landscaping, deck, or patio project.

- Study your schoolwork by using graph paper and mapping out ideas.

Your thoughts: Who do you know who is strong in the area of Visual/Spatial Intelligence? Explain.

_____

_____

_____

_____

_____

_____

Verbal/Linguistic Intelligence

These audial learners use words and language to convey their ideas. They have highly developed auditory skills and are generally elegant speakers. They think in words rather than pictures.

Possible career interests: Journalist, writer, teacher, lawyer, politician, translator.

Suggested action steps to further develop these skills:

- Read a book each week.

- Stay informed about the actions of political leaders.

- Write a book. Protect it. Publish it.

- Sign up for membership at www.dictionary.com to receive, via e-mail, the definition of one new word each day.

Your thoughts: Who do you know who is strong in the area of Verbal/Linguistic Intelligence? Explain.

_____

_____

_____

_____

_____

_____

Logical/Mathematical Intelligence

These learners have the ability to use reason, logic, and numbers with ease. They think conceptually in logical and numerical patterns to make connections between pieces of information. These learners will always use scientific explanations and real facts when debating a topic.

Possible career interests: Scientist, engineer, computer programmer, researcher, accountant, mathematician.

Suggested action steps to further develop these skills:

- Design your own computer games.

- Practice your math skills.

Your thoughts: Who do you know who is strong in the area of Logical/Mathematical Intelligence? Explain.

_____

_____

_____

_____

_____

_____

_____

_____

_____

Musical/Rhythmic Intelligence

Musical learners have the ability to appreciate and pattern their lives with the guidance of music. They think in sounds, rhythms, and patterns and are very opinionated about what they hear.

Possible Career Interests: Musician, music teacher, disc jockey, singer, composer.

Suggested action steps to further develop these skills:

- Find part-time work in your area of interest to gain more skills.

- Make CDs for friends and family members.

Your thoughts: Who do you know who is strong in the area of Musical/Rhythmic Intelligence? Explain.

_____

_____

_____

_____

_____

_____

_____

_____

Interpersonal Intelligence

This learner has the ability to relate and understand others better than most people. They try to see things from other people's perspectives in order to understand how they think and feel. They often have an incredible ability to sense the feelings, intentions, and motivations of others. They are great organizers, although they sometimes resort to manipulation.

Possible Career Interests: Counselor, salesperson, sales manager, politician, businessperson.

Suggested action steps to further develop these skills:

- Read self-help books to gain a deeper understanding of human behaviors.

- Apply this knowledge to help you understand people close to you.

- Practice being in integrity with your thoughts, feelings, and actions to become a role model to others.

- Practice and study the art of listening.

Your thoughts: Who do you know who is strong in the area of Interpersonal Intelligence? Explain.

_____

_____

_____

_____

_____

_____

_____

_____

_____

_____

_____

_____

_____

Intrapersonal Intelligence

This learner has the ability to dig deep within him or herself and understand his or her innermost thoughts. He or she tries to interpret dreams, relationships with others, and life paths.

Possible Career Interests: Researcher, theorist, philosopher.

Suggested action steps to further develop these skills:

- Learn to understand yourself.

- Study philosophy and great thinkers of the past, such as Aristotle, Dalton, Bacon, Socrates.

- Write down your dreams, and see if you can figure out what they mean.

Your thoughts: Who do you know who is strong in the area of Intrapersonal Intelligence? Explain.

_____

_____

_____

_____

_____

_____

Naturalistic Intelligence

This learner operates best when working outdoors. Creativity flows as soon as this learner is exposed to fresh air.

Possible Career Interests: Outdoor researcher, nature reporter, archeologist, park ranger, athlete.

Suggested action steps that will help further develop these skills:

- Go for early morning runs or hikes outdoors, and see if the activity helps stimulate your thoughts.

- Take a drive and look at the beautiful scenery. How does looking at nature make you feel?

- If you live near the ocean, sit on the shore and watch the waves. Think of the amazing depth of the water, and imagine the life moving beneath the surface. What else comes to your mind when you think of the unseen?

Your thoughts: Who do you know who is strong in the area of Naturalistic Intelligence? Explain.

_____

_____

_____

_____

_____

_____

Follow-up with the
Multiple Intelligence Theory

Discuss which intelligences you have developed more fully than others. Identify how you learn best. Are you a visual learner, a person who likes to see things in front of you? Are you an auditory learner, one who takes in new information by listening? Do you learn best by touching and experimenting through physical movement? Or do you learn best by reading about something?

1. I learn best by:

_____
_____
_____
_____
_____
_____
_____
_____
_____
_____

2. The intelligences that I have highly developed are:

_____
_____
_____
_____
_____
_____
_____
_____
_____

3. This means my strengths are:

_____
_____
_____
_____
_____
_____
_____
_____
_____

4. This means my weaknesses are:

_____
_____
_____
_____
_____
_____
_____
_____
_____

Put your new knowledge into practice

1. Using the Multiple Intelligence Test, what did you learn about yourself?

_____
_____
_____

2. How do your different intelligences blend together in certain activities you do?

_____
_____
_____
_____

3. Which of your underdeveloped intelligences would you like to develop further?

_____

_____

_____

_____

4. What are your next steps toward developing them?

_____

_____

_____

_____

5. I would like to work on the following intelligences, and here is how:

_____

_____

_____

_____

_____

_____

_____

_____

_____

Review

This section will allow you to take a closer look at each of the different intelligences. Look at your most developed intelligence to see if your career interest matches your skills.

-   For parents and teachers, think of how you can work with others using your knowledge of these intelligences. What insight can this information give you into your own life?

-   For teenagers, this section can help you further develop intelligences that are less developed, and it will help you gain understanding of your strong areas.

Extension Exercises

How would you remedy each of the following situations?

- As a student, what feedback could you give to another student who is upset because his history class is boring? It seems that all the class entails is reading through the text. In this scenario, what could you do to help?

- You are very good at math, but you are not challenged at school because others in your math class are struggling. What can you do to be sure that you continue to study math that challenges your mind?

- You know that your Verbal/Linguistic Intelligence is underdeveloped, yet you excel in the area of Logical/Mathematical Intelligence. You are struggling with your chemistry word problems. What can you do?

PART TWO

Ten Top-Secret Lessons

Test Your Current Knowledge on Attitude

Now that you have had a chance to study your intelligences and you understand in more depth how you learn, it is time to move toward mastery of the Ten Top Secret Lessons. Considering that your behavior is derived from your attitude, this first lesson, a lesson about attitude, can be described as the cornerstone to success in anyone's life. How you act toward life and the situations you face will determine your altitude in life.

Two people facing the same tragedy can react with two completely different attitudes. Imagine being told that your services were no longer needed at work and you were laid off. One person might take the news very hard and think their life were over. Another person could see this news as an opportunity to grow and find a new job where they could perhaps advance to a higher level. How is your attitude?

> Human beings can alter their lives by altering their attitudes of mind.
>
> *William James (1842–1910), American*
> *psychologist and philosopher trained in medicine*

- Parents and teachers should think about the attitudes they convey at home versus the attitudes they convey while at work. How are they different?

- Teenagers should think about the attitudes they have at school versus the attitudes they present at home. How are they different?

1. What does the word "attitude" mean to you?

_____

_____

_____

_____

_____

2. Do you think you have a good attitude most of the time? Why or why not?

_____

_____

_____

_____

_____

3. How important do you think attitude is in your daily life?

_____

_____

_____

_____

_____

4. What is the difference between reacting aggressively and responding caringly to a situation?

_____

_____

_____

_____

_____

5. How does your attitude affect your results?

_____

_____

_____

_____

_____

_____

6. What happens to your results when you think negative thoughts?

_____

_____

_____

_____

_____

_____

_____

_____

7. Can someone else affect your attitude? Why or why not?

_____

_____

_____

_____

_____

_____

8. Can your attitude affect the world around you? If so, how?

_____

_____

_____

_____

_____

_____

9. Can your attitude affect your health? If so, how?

_____

_____

_____

_____

_____

_____

10. Does a person with a good attitude ever use blame when things do not go their way? Why not?

_____

_____

_____

_____

_____

_____

_____

_____

Why is a winning attitude so important for a rewarding life?

I have missed more than nine thousand shots in my career. I have lost almost three hundred games. On twenty-six occasions I have been entrusted to take the game winning shot...and I missed. I have failed over and over and over again in my life. And that's precisely why I succeed.

—Michael Jordan, American
basketball player

Think
About This!

- For parents and teachers, when you are working through this lesson, think of the changes you would like to make to your attitude. It is hard to always have a good attitude, but it is not impossible. Do you have a good attitude at all times? Think of the how you act when your favorite bagel shop runs out of bacon and you know your sandwich just will not be the same. Think about how you act when someone cuts you off as you're driving home from the office. Take an honest look at your attitude.

- For teenagers, dissecting attitude is a good place to start because having a good attitude will determine your altitude in life. Think about how others might perceive you. Do they think you are an easygoing person? Or do people say you are difficult to get along with? The key to having a good attitude is to learn to adapt to all personality types so you can easily get along with anyone. This just takes practice.

Lesson

What Is Attitude?

Attitude has been described by many successful leaders as the most important word in this and any other language. Everything you do and all that you become is determined by your mental attitude. It is the foundation of your success. When you give up control of your attitude to what you think is a negative situation, you will react negatively. When you react negatively to any situation, you lose. On the other hand, you can choose to be objective and respond to the situation in an appropriate manner. The end result of these two approaches gives way to results that are miles apart.

Reacting with Aggression vs. Responding with Empathy

Aggressive Response: Imagine someone walks past you and casts a disdainful look in your direction. What do you think? How does receiving that look make you feel? What do you do?

If you opt to react in an aggressive manner you might return the disdainful look. Perhaps you would even shout something negative at the person. This reaction could result in a physical argument that in turn could become a physical fight. No one wins when they react aggressively to a situation, and yet, this is the way most people deal with a challenge.

Respond with Empathy: Consider the possibility that the mean look was not meant for you. Perhaps the fellow casting the look had something on his mind, and the nasty look had nothing to do with you. How could you find out? You could respond kindly and ask sincerely and with an open mind, "Are you okay? Can I help you with something?" The person will see that you are not responding aggressively. This will, in turn, stop their aggression.

The Power Your Attitude Has on Your Life

To attain the results that you really want in life, you must be in total control. To be in control, you must understand the power your attitude has over your results. Others can detect your attitude within a few minutes of first meeting you. Do you want to always make a good first impression?

Did you know that your attitude casts an aura of energy that can be photographed? This type of photography is called Kurlian photography. So, if you are in a bad mood, you'd better believe that everyone is able to detect it. Trust me; even your dog can feel it.

1. **Have you ever noticed your pet react differently to you when you were in a bad mood? What did you notice?**

_____

_____

_____

_____

_____

Your attitude toward the world will determine the world's attitude toward you. Have you ever noticed that when you feel hostile toward a certain person, that person usually feels the same way about you? On the flipside, if you really enjoy someone's company and get along well with them, that person usually feels the same way about you. Like people and like things attract like people and like things. You attract all the situations in your life.

By maintaining control of the way you think, feel, and act, you cause good things to happen to you in your life. When you think good thoughts like "I am so happy about…" or "Wow, I am so grateful for…" and then act in integrity with your thoughts, others will see that you are genuine. You can actually magnetize good things to come your way through positive thinking.

2. Have you ever noticed that when something good happens, the situation snowballs and more and more good things happen? Provide some examples of a good day that just kept getting better.

_____

_____

_____

_____

_____

3. Now, consider a day when things seemed really bad. Did the same thing happen? Was there a snowball effect of negative events? Provide an example of a bad day that just kept getting worse.

_____

_____

_____

_____

_____

So, how does this happen? It all begins with your attitude. Your attitude is a composite of your thoughts, feelings, and actions. If you spend time thinking, "I am so mad about this" or "I can't believe I messed that up," believe it or not, your attitude will attract even more misfortune.

Review

Concepts of a Winning Attitude

Give your opinion of each of the statements listed below. Explain why you either agree or disagree with each statement.

1. "Everything can be taken away from a person, except their attitude." —Viktor Frankl

   _____

   _____

   _____

   _____

   _____

2. Attitude is the most powerful word, and it relates to all areas of our lives.

   _____

   _____

   _____

   _____

   _____

3. When you surrender control of your attitude, you react aggressively to a situation instead of responding caringly.

   _____

   _____

   _____

   _____

   _____

   _____

4. When we respond caringly to a situation, we will come out as winners. Explain why.

_____

_____

_____

_____

_____

5. Your attitude can be controlled and understood. It is not easy to do this, but it is possible if you work at it diligently.

_____

_____

_____

_____

_____

6. Your attitude is an expression of all three parts of your personality: your thoughts, feelings, and actions.

_____

_____

_____

_____

_____

7. Attitude and results are inseparable. Your thoughts, feelings, and actions therefore control your results.

_____

_____

_____

_____

_____

8. A person's life is what he or she thinks of it.

_____

_____

_____

_____

_____

9. You can choose to look at the positive or negative side of a situation, but you can only concentrate on either the negative or positive at once.

_____

_____

_____

_____

_____

10. If you think negative thoughts, you will get negative results.

_____

_____

_____

_____

_____

11. If you think positive thoughts, we will get positive results.

_____

_____

_____

_____

_____

12. Winners are very rare because most people give up too easily or too soon, sometimes just before they hit gold.

_____

_____

_____

_____

_____

13. Another person cannot upset or affect you without your permission.

_____

_____

_____

_____

_____

14. Winners never blame others when things do not go their way.

_____

_____

_____

_____

15. Winners know that they are never given a problem that they cannot solve.

_____

_____

_____

_____

16. When winners get knocked down, they get right back up and keep their eyes on their goal. Losing is the act of falling down and staying down. The minute you stand up and try again, you are a winner.

_____

_____

_____

_____

17. Everything happens according to a Law of the Universe, or for a reason.

_____

_____

_____

_____

18. Your attitude toward others determines the attitude others respond with.

_____

_____

_____

_____

19. Your mental attitude affects your health.

_____

_____

_____

_____

20. Winners believe they will attain unlimited success even when
    it appears they will not.

_____

_____

_____

_____

Remember This

- **You choose your thoughts, which form ideas.** Thought energy is the most potent form of energy. You can think, "I am so happy" or "I am so upset." You choose your thoughts, and it is you who will attract more fortune or misfortune to your life. It all depends on what happens in your mind. Only you know what you are thinking, so be careful.

- **Ideas stream into your emotional mind and cause you to have feelings.** You will either feel good about certain thoughts you have, or you will feel bad. When you have a decision to make, notice how you are feeling. When you feel badly about the decision, you know you are attracting more negativity to your life, and you will know that this is probably not the best decision you could make. Conversely, when you feel good, more good is on the way. Your feelings are an internal signal. They let you know if you are attracting good things or bad things, and they can be used as your own Global Positioning System.

- **The way you feel determines the actions you take.** Ideas and emotions are expressed in your actions. If, for example, you are feeling good about a test you're about to take, you will probably run into the classroom, sit down, and take the test with confidence. On the other hand, if you are feeling badly about the test because you barely studied, you will walk to your desk, sit with your head down, and probably cause more anxiety to yourself because of your bad attitude.

- **Your actions produce a reaction that in turn causes your results.** You can choose to either react positively or negatively to a situation. The results of each reaction are poles apart. Therefore, attitude and results are inseparable.

Can you provide an example of when you knew your attitude affected your results? Give an example of a good result and of a bad result. How would you change your attitude in the future, to change your results?

_____

_____

_____

So, Why Do the Thoughts I Think Matter?

A person's life is what their thoughts make of it.
*Ralph Waldo Emerson, essayist, author, and poet whose teachings
directly affected the New Thought Movement in the 1800s.*

We can choose to look at either the positive or the negative side of any situation, but notice how a person can only focus on one of these ways of thinking at a time. Those who are deemed winners are aware of negative ways of thinking, but they only focus on the positive. When a negative thought creeps into your mind, the best way to get rid of it is to shout out "switch" and replace it with a positive thought.

If you think negative thoughts, you will get negative results. If you think positive, you will attract positive results.

Notice that when someone has a winning attitude, everyone around them benefits. Their attitude is contagious. A winner may get knocked down, but they never stay down. A winner sees obstacles as learning experiences. They remain focused on their goals and continue to pursue them.

Extension
Exercises

1. Go home tonight and carefully monitor your behavior. If you get into a confrontation with a family member, watch what you do. Are you able to respond positively instead of reacting negatively? Write down what happens, what you do, and what you learn from it. How can you make the situation better next time?

_____

_____

_____

_____

_____

_____

_____

_____

_____

2. In general, what have you noticed about your attitude? Do you think you have a good one? Is there someone you know whose attitude you like better? What can you do to improve your attitude?

_____

_____

_____

_____

_____

_____

_____

_____

_____

3. Have you noticed that you sometimes think negatively? What limiting thoughts have you had? Have you been able to *switch* these negative thoughts to positive ones? Practice switching, and see if it gets easier to think positively.

---

4. Do you agree with what Charles Swindall is saying in this passage about the importance of a good attitude?

The longer I live, the more I realize the impact of attitude on life. Attitude, to me, is more important than facts. It is more important than the past, than education, than money, than circumstances, than failures, than successes, than what other people think or say or do. It is more important than appearance, giftedness, or skill. It will make or break a company ... a church ... a home. The remarkable thing is we have a choice every day regarding the attitude we will embrace for that day. We cannot change our past ... we cannot change the fact that people will act in a certain way. We cannot change the inevitable. The only thing we can do is play on the one string we have, and that is our attitude ... I am convinced that life is 10 percent of what happens to me, and 90 percent of how I react to it. And so it is with you ... we are in charge of our attitude.[1]

Charles R.Swindoll, American Writer and Clergyman

---

1   Swindoll, R. Charles, Thinkexist.com

5. Can you identify a time when your attitude led to a result you did not want? (Example: You spoke disrespectfully to someone, and a negative consequence occurred.)

_____

_____

_____

6. Can you identify a time when your attitude provided a result you wanted?

(Example: Your friend was angry with you. She let you know that your actions upset her feelings, so you were able to apologize and fix the situation).

_____

_____

_____

Put it into Practice

Now that you understand the importance of a good attitude vs. a bad attitude, see if you can help someone with a bad attitude switch out of it. Choose one friend/family member who does not appear to be smiling, and see if you can turn their attitude around. It may mean that you have to be extra nice, fun, and friendly, but we know that good attitudes are contagious. You get bonus points if you actually prevent a conflict or argument by switching their attitude. Write about how you changed someone's attitude.

_____

_____

_____

_____

_____

_____

_____

_____

_____

_____

Test Your Current Knowledge of the Mind

Opportunity thinking is an art form.

Mark Victor Hansen, coauthor of
the Chicken Soup for the Soul series.

Now that you have had a chance to take a closer look at your attitude, the next step is to learn how you can control your attitude and your results by using your mind. This lesson is extremely powerful. You will begin to see that you no longer need to look for answers outside of yourself. Everything you need to know about your life and your destiny, you already know. You will need to go to a quiet place so you will be able to hear the stillness in your mind. Then, the answers will begin to flow at a rapid rate.

- Parents and teachers should think about the difference between their minds and their brains. Do you believe that your thoughts can really affect results? How often do you use your gut feelings to direct you in life?

- Teenagers should think about instinct and where it comes from. When you attain unfavorable results, do you think they could be caused by your thinking that, or do you blame the results on outside factors?

1. Do you know how ideas come into your mind?

_____

_____

_____

_____

_____

_____

2. Do you know why some people continuously attract negative results?

_____

_____

_____

3. Do you think that your thoughts can affect your mood and body?

_____

_____

_____

4. Do you know the difference between a gut feeling and a feeling that has emotion attached to it?

_____

_____

_____

5. What are the higher faculties of your mind?

_____

_____

_____

6. How can you use your will to get what you want?

_____

_____

_____

7. Do you know what it means to think on autopilot?

_____

_____

_____

8. Do you believe there is much more to the world than what your eyes can see?

_____

_____

_____

What is your mind, and how does it control your destiny?

Think
About This!

- Parents and teachers should think about the power of the mind. How can you further develop and use this power? How will you use your conscious mind to create your goals, and in turn, how will you work on your subconscious mind to eliminate habits that hold you back? Do you want to learn more about the awesome powers of your subconscious mind? Most people, once they begin to study, are amazed by the how much they thought they knew. They then realize there is so much more to uncover and understand.

Motivational speaker Bob Proctor has spent the past forty years studying the mind and teaching people how it works. He will tell you that no person or circumstance will cause you to think thoughts that you do not choose to think. You are responsible for your thoughts, and these thoughts will determine the results in your life.

- Teenagers should know that they will have a much easier time reaching their goals than adults because the teenage mind has formed fewer habits than the adult mind.

An educated person is not one who has acquired general or specialized knowledge; an educated person is one who has so developed the faculties of their mind that they can acquire anything they want, or its equivalent, without violating the rights of others.

Napoleon Hill (1883–1970), American author
who was one of the first producers of personal
development material. His book Think and Grow
Rich *is one of the best-selling books of all time.*

How will you plan to bring your goals to fruition at this age when the world is so full of opportunity for you? How will you learn to use your subconscious mind to help you live a more peaceful life?

What visual comes to mind when you are asked, "What is your mind?" Draw a picture in the cloud of what you think your mind looks like.

Before you can learn to train your mind to get the results you desire, you must have a picture in your mind of what your mind is. Your mind is not your brain. Your brain is the storage container, and your mind is the energy that flows within it. It is the power that flows through you. Your mind is your seat of consciousness, your thoughts and feelings. Your mind is energy that comes from your Higher Being, which every living thing is connected to. This energy cannot be destroyed. It has always existed, and it is always working. Once you understand the power that your mind holds, it will be easier for you to use it.

Review

Check Your Understanding

If you understand that your mind is not your brain, then do you understand what your mind is? Your mind is energy that you get from the Universal Consciousness. This energy has always existed and always will. The arrows emanating from this person's head shows the energy that the mind can create. You can actually photograph your energy using a process called Kurlian photography. Some people can even read your energy or aura. It appears to them as different colors, depending on the mood of the person being read.

Extension
Exercise

See if you can find someone who can read auras, or the energy fields that surrounds people. (This is something that you can do when you visit the New Age Spiritual Center in Sedona, Arizona.) Record your findings on reading auras.

_____

_____

_____

_____

_____

_____

_____

_____

_____

_____

_____

_____

_____

_____

Lessons on
the Mind

Note: This lesson has three sections labeled A, B, and C. In Lesson A, you will learn about the Conscious or Thinking Mind, Lesson B will teach you about the Subconscious or Emotional Mind, and Lesson C will focus on the body.

Eliminate Confusion and Bring Order to Your Mind for Guaranteed Results.

This diagram has been used for many years in live seminars given by Bob Proctor and LifeSuccess Productions. It has helped many youth, adults, and business owners attain more positive results simply by gaining a new perspective of their thinking. Think of this diagram as a picture of you and your mind.[1]

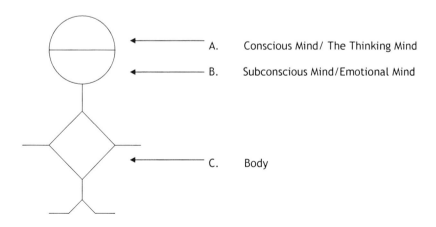

A.	Conscious Mind/ The Thinking Mind
B.	Subconscious Mind/Emotional Mind
C.	Body

---

1 This concept of the mind and body originated with the late Dr. Thurman Fleet of San Antonio, Texas, circa 1934. Dr. Fleet was the founder of Concept Therapy

A. The Conscious Mind, or the Thinking Mind

This is the part of the mind you're using when you are consciously doing something like reading, studying, learning, solving problems, or playing sports.

We can use our minds and thoughts to view the world and our surroundings in two different ways. One way is quite limited; this is the way most people live their lives. They live by using their five senses.

For example, someone can live their entire life relying solely on sight or sound. And why wouldn't we use sight or sound? We were given these gifts at birth, so what could possibly be wrong with this idea? This idea is so interesting to talk about. For when we study science, we learn that there is so much more to this world than that which our eyes can see.

The desk I am sitting at is really a bunch of molecules all joined together. If we were to look at the desk through a microscope, we would see something that didn't look much like our interpretation of a desk. In the same regard, there are some sounds that humans cannot hear, but some animals have access to these pitches.

Therefore, a person who relies entirely upon that which they can see with their naked eyes and hear with their ears must be aware that there is much more to what they are seeing and hearing.

Sometimes, the things we can see and hear can be altered or expanded by using higher faculties of the mind. This is the second way that you can view the world with your mind. This method is much more resourceful, and it can be practiced and sharpened for better results over time.

For example, begin the goal achievement process by first of all using *the will*, where we can keep our vision and goals in our minds until we move them into physical form. We can use *reasoning* to guess whether a certain idea is best suited for us, *imagination* to expand and dream about our goals, *concentration* to hold our goals on the screen of our mind for a sustained time and ensure that our thoughts do not waver under difficulties or stress, *memory* to make connections with ideas we have learned in the past, *intuition* to allow our inner instincts to guide us, and *perception* to gain another view of something.

Did you know that when we go to sleep, our conscious mind also goes to sleep? We become that which we think about. Your attitude and conscious thinking are the main cause to your future success. It separates you from the animal kingdom. This part of your mind can accept or reject any new information or idea. How powerful is that?

Suggested action step to further develop these skills

Explain how people live their lives using their five senses. Give five examples of ways you see people around you making decisions based on their five senses.

The Conscious/Thinking Mind Contains the Five Senses

Sight: I see that my grades are all Cs. That must be the only grade I am capable of achieving. Therefore, I will study just enough to barely scrape by with Cs.

Touch:

Taste:

Hearing:

Smell:

Your Six Intellectual Factors

The Higher Faculties of the Mind

When asked to list the higher faculties of the mind, most people have no idea what they're being asked, and they will stare at you blankly.

Go and ask your teacher or your parents and see what he or she says. Not many people know what they are. How can we develop these faculties if we don't even know they exist? Your higher faculties are the most powerful part of your mind, especially as you learn to develop and use them. These faculties can sense things that our five senses cannot, simply because they cannot be touched, tasted, heard, smelled, or seen. They can only be felt by an inner feeling or knowledge within the depths of your mind.

You may have heard that we only use 10 percent of our brain power while the other 90 percent remains inactive. Imagine what heights you could reach if you focused on developing the higher faculties of your mind.

Perception is your point of view. This factor can be altered at will which means that you can always see two sides to a situation, but it takes the will and some effort to switch your way of thinking to see another side of something. If you are having a problem or disagreement with someone, try to look at the issue at hand through their eyes to see a different point of view, not just your own.

Reasoning is the ability to think. Having this faculty makes us different from other members of the animal kingdom; they do not have the

ability to reason. When you use your will to create activity in your mind, you can attract your goals if you are able to sustain your positive thinking. Just by being focused, you have the power to think powerful ideas. And by using your will, you can bring these ideas to you.

Michael Dooley, a teacher from the movie *The Secret*, reminds us of a very powerful concept that our "thoughts become things," which means that we manifest what we think about, so we need to be extremely careful about what we think about.

The will is the understanding that each idea has a certain pattern. The will gives you the ability to concentrate on and increase the amplitude (the height of the wave) of the vibration of your thoughts, making them very powerful. Use the will to lock into an idea and block out all other distractions. Also, using the will allows you to focus your mind on the things you want. You can get on the same wavelength as your goals and desires, and then you can work to attract them to you.

Decreased amplitude = weak thoughts
Increased amplitude by using the will = powerful thoughts

The important point to remember is that sometimes when your goals or dreams seem far away, you might believe in your heart that they will always remain dreams. You may convince yourself that these goals and dreams will never become reality. It is essential that you truly believe in your heart that you will have the things you want. This will be difficult at first, but grasping the concept will be the key to your success. Use your will to keep your eyes on your goals and eliminate doubts and fears.

Memory is something you can develop with practice. There is no such thing as a bad memory. However, just like your muscles, if your memory is not used, it can become weak. When you do not exercise the muscles in your body, they lose strength. This is exactly what happens when you are not practicing your memory. Treat your mind with as much care and consideration

as you would your body, as they are very much connected. The more practice you give this faculty, the stronger it will become.

Imagination takes you to a place no one but you has ever been. All great inventions are created in two separate places: the mind of the inventor and the physical world when the inventor creates it. Let your mind soar, and take note of the things you think about when you dream. When it comes to your dreams, stay focused. They can become reality with effort and persistence.

Intuition is a mental tool that is instilled within each of us at birth. It gives us answers, by picking up the energy or a certain vibe or

feeling from another person. We can even read a person's energy over the telephone. Sometimes we feel we just know the answer, or we have a gut feeling. That is our intuition at work, and we must learn to develop it. With practice, we can learn to trust our intuition and become confident with that which we feel or know. Then, we can move confidently toward that which we want.

Sometimes our dreams give us answers to things we want to know, and sometimes this is really our subconscious mind speaking to us.

Review

Complete the following exercise to demonstrate that you understand the six faculties of your mind. Remember that the faculties of the mind are in your conscious, or thinking, mind.

The Conscious Mind Contains the Six Intellectual Factors

Imagination

Your imagination is unique to you and takes you to a place no one else has ever gone.

Write about a time you made use of your imagination with a goal.

_____
_____
_____
_____

Reason

We can use reasoning to make an educated guess as to whether a specific idea is something that we agree or disagree with.

Write about a time you used your reasoning factor.

_____
_____
_____
_____

Perception

Everything we look at with our eyes has different sides to it. What we see with our eyes, someone else might see in an entirely different way. Try to see through other people's eyes and observe different points of view.

Explain a time when someone you knew could not see something the same way you saw it.

_____
_____
_____
_____

Intuition

Our intuition is our inner guidance system; it works by picking up the energy around us. If something feels good to us, it is usually a good indicator that we are moving on the right track. Our inner guidance is picking up on the good energy. If something feels bad, we are probably going against our inner guidance system and feeling the negative energy. **Explain a time when you used your intuition or inner guidance system to help you make a decision.**

_____

_____

_____

_____

The Will

The will can be used to help you form a mental image of your goals. It gives you the ability to concentrate on your goals and make your thoughts more powerful. When you are writing a paper, it takes will to get started and to remain focused on finishing. In another example, it takes will to get up and go to the gym to exercise.

Explain a time when you used your will to stay focused on something that you really wanted and blocked out all other distractions.

_____

_____

_____

_____

Memory

There is no such thing as a bad memory; there are just memories that lack practice. Explain a time when you were able to further develop this mental muscle.

_____

_____

_____

There are many things that your body can sense that do not exist in a physical state. However, that does not mean that these things do not exist. Your higher faculties help you sense things that are in non-physical form—things that exist, but cannot be see with the human eye.

Use of the Will

There is a part of your subconscious mind that you can control with your will. You can be sitting in front of the television on autopilot, and with the use of your will, you can be thinking or focusing on something else. You can stop negative thoughts from entering your subconscious mind just by using your will. This is an amazing concept. You have total control of your subconscious mind, as it is you who controls what goes in and what stays out. This takes lots of practice. Are you able to use your will to get the results you are looking for?

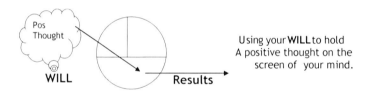

Using your **WILL** to hold
A positive thought on the
screen of your mind.

**To Understand the Unseen Part of your Conscious or Thinking Mind,
Look at This!**

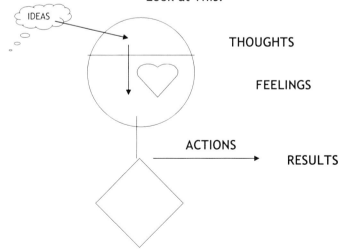

What we can see, things in the physical realm, and what we cannot see, things in the nonphysical realm, are linked. Thoughts enter our minds from the non-physical realm in the form of ideas. These ideas give us feelings. When we pair emotions with our ideas and act on them, we can bring them into physical form. This is exactly how Thomas Edison created the lightbulb. Had the idea never entered his mind, he could not have created it. Imagine that every idea that has ever existed has always been here. We can tap into these ideas when we focus our mind. Then we bring the idea to physical form with action. This is where results come from.

What ideas have come to you in a flash? What have you done with these ideas?

_____

_____

_____

_____

_____

_____

_____

_____

_____

_____

_____

_____

To understand how your mind operates, you must understand all three of these planes (the subconscious mind, the conscious mind and the body) and how your mind interacts with them to create your results. An idea floating around in the cosmic consciousness enters your mind; it can either be accepted or rejected by your conscious mind. If the idea is accepted and given energy, power, and direction from your emotional mind, then it can be brought to physical form.

If there is something you really want, just take some time, relax, and let ideas flow into your mind. Keep a pencil handy, and when an idea that you like hits your conscious thinking, give it energy with your heart.

The next thing you must do is learn to understand your subconscious mind, as it will try to knock you off course. Any time we introduce a new idea to the mind, it takes some time for your subconscious mind to accept it.

> Any idea that is held in the mind that is either feared or revered will begin at once to clothe itself in the most convenient and appropriate physical forms available.
>
> *Andrew Carnegie (1883–1919), Scottish-born*
> *American who was a major philanthropist and*
> *the second richest man after John D. Rockefeller.*

Review

Remember that you can attract positive and negative ideas and situations. If you are worried about not making the basketball team, you may attract an undesirable outcome when the coach reads the team roster. The same holds true if you have a positive attitude about your studies; you more than likely will attain good grades.

Write about something you cannot seem to get out of your mind. What goals, dreams, or ideas do you think about?

_____

_____

_____

_____

_____

_____

_____

_____

_____

_____

_____

_____

_____

_____

Analyze the thoughts or ideas from the previous question. Are there any negative ideas or thoughts invading your mind? We all have them. Write them down so you can see what they are and learn how to work toward managing them. Remember, even your fears will come true if you are always thinking about them. Get them out in the open.

_____

_____

_____

_____

_____

_____

_____

_____

Once you have created this list, take a red pen or a thick marker and draw a big X through it. Yes, you read that correctly.

Exactly like John Keating, Robin Williams's character in *Dead Poets Society*, a man who had his students rip out the beginning pages of *Norton's Anthology of English Literature*, I am asking you to mark a big X through something that will only hold you back.

Everyone has fears, but to constantly think of what might go wrong will only draw negativity toward us. It will only attract more of what we do not want. We will need to train our minds to remain optimistic and positive even in the most difficult situations.

B. The Subconscious Mind/Automatic Thinking

This part of your mind accepts whatever enters it. It is the most powerful part of your body. This is so because many of your body parts function on autopilot which is really just your subconscious mind at work. Any idea that you accept into your conscious mind also goes into your subconscious mind and becomes an integral part of who you are. These fixed ideas turn into habits. Ideas are easily solidified here, especially when they are surrounded by intense emotion.

For example, imagine yourself sitting in front of the television. You are not thinking about anything in particular; you are simply watching the TV. Your mind is in a submissive state. It's not working to control what goes in and what stays out. All the things you are seeing are going directly into your subconscious mind. If you are watching a scary movie, your mind in this submissive state doesn't distinguish between fact and fiction. It actually believes you are experiencing the horror first hand. Your body reacts by sweating, and your heart rate goes up. These things are done automatically. Your subconscious mind thinks you are actually experiencing what your eyes are seeing.

The same thing happens when you are eating. Notice how your mind operates when you sit down and begin to eat your dinner. At this point, anyone's thoughts can go straight into your subconscious mind. Be careful with who you surround yourself with, as their thoughts can affect your mood.

Here is a final thought. The same thing can happen if you are in a room full of people. Imagine yourself in a submissive state in a classroom or at the office. When your mind enters this submissive state—when you're not actively thinking about anything. If someone is thinking negative thoughts, these thoughts affect each and every person in the room. It is important to remain aware of this fact because sometimes you get really angry or irritated when you are around someone, and you cannot figure out why. You will now know that you are feeling their negative thinking, and it does not feel good. This is an easy problem to solve. When you feel bad around someone, walk away.

Outside negativity
can control your feelings.

Subconscious Mind

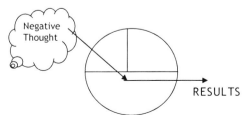

To learn more about the subconscious mind and studying your dreams, read *The Power of Your Subconscious Mind* by Dr. Joseph Murphy. Murphy (1898–1981) was an author who lectured and counseled people worldwide for over fifty years.

C. The Body

Did you know that your body inherits what your mind expresses? If you have healthy thoughts, then your body will be in the best environment to be healthy. Conversely, if you tend to dwell on negative situations, that can actually put stress on your body, and can cause dis-ease in your body.

You must have heard that stress is contributes to most illnesses. Everyone faces stress, but how you let it affect you will determine the health of your body and mind. A healthy dose of optimism can go a long way while coping with life's stressful situations.

Remember that if you are thinking healthy, positive thoughts, they will be reflected in your body.

Healthy thinking = healthy body cells

A Note About Body Image

Note that your body may not look like your best friend's, the guy you are working out next to, or your neighbor's, but it is perfect for you so long as you are thinking positive thoughts.

Review

1. Be able to draw and label the stick person from page 58—concept of the mind and body—without looking at your notes.

2. Be able to list the five senses and the six higher faculties.

3. Single out one of the higher faculties and practice developing it.

Extension
Exercises

1. To further develop your intuition, see if you can guess who is calling you on the phone before you answer it. Go with your first thought, and then see who it is. This will take practice before you begin to guess correctly. Be prepared to explain your accuracy.

2. To develop your memory, go online and Google "memory games." You will find some games that you can play that will strengthen this faculty of your mind.

3. To aid your perception, try to look at things from someone else's point of view in a conversation. Is this easy or difficult to do?

Test Your Current Knowledge
of the Laws of the Universe

Your next step in this program is to take the power of your mind and sharpen your higher faculties from the previous chapter so you can begin to attain predictable results. Everything you need to know is within your own mind, and once you learn to master life and living in harmony with these laws, everything will seem much easier for you.

- Parents and teachers need to think about their knowledge of the Laws of the Universe. Do you understand what they are and how they work? Do you believe they can work? If you are skeptical, pick up the book *Working with the Laws* by Raymond Holliwell. It will help you gain belief in that which we cannot see.

- Teenagers and students need to think about the areas of their lives in which they could use some assistance. Once you understand the Laws of the Universe, you should be able to view your challenges in a new light. When you understand these laws, there will be no obstacle that can hold you back. You will achieve your goals. You won't know when the achievement will take place, but if you work in harmony with the laws, success is inevitable.

1. **Have you seen the movie *The Secret*?**

_____

_____

_____

_____

_____

_____

_____

2. Can you explain The Law of Attraction?

_____

_____

_____

_____

_____

_____

_____

3. Do you know that there are many laws that can be used to
   help you attain your goals?

_____

_____

_____

_____

_____

_____

_____

4. Can you name any of these laws?

_____

_____

_____

_____

_____

_____

LESSON THREE

How will the laws of the universe change your life immediately?

Think
About This!

- Parents and teachers, if you have heard of The Law of Attraction, you might wonder how it actually works. There is much more to this law than simply thinking positive thoughts and waiting for good things to happen to you. If somewhere deep inside you do not believe that you will achieve your goal, that goal will escape you. Once you fully understand The Law of Attraction, another skill must be realized. You must be in harmony or rapport with your goal. If you have self-doubt, you will not be in harmony, and your goal will remain out of reach. Learn how to line up with your desires in this chapter. Doing this will take practice. Then one day, you will be amazed when everything lines up and goes your way. It will be like one of those days when you hit all green lights on your way home. On those days, you are working with the Laws.

- Teenagers and students, as you practice the laws in this chapter, take note of The Law of Cause and Effect. Everything you do matters greatly. You matter. You can create significant change in this world by the actions that you take. Think about what change you would like to make in this world, and create a plan of action. You can cause a ripple that will affect the whole world. Decide what it will be, and take action. You have the rest of your life to make a difference. Why not start now?

Lessons

1. The Law of Attraction and Vibration

2. The Law of Polarity

3. The Law of Rhythm

4. The Law of Relativity

5. The Law of Cause and Effect

6. The Law of Physical Manifestation

1. The Law of Attraction and Vibration

If you've watched *The Secret*, then you know all about this law. This law explains why bad things happen when we think bad thoughts, and why good things just keep getting better when we think positive thoughts.

How exactly does this happen? Because we are spiritual beings, our thoughts attract other like thoughts and actions. Our thoughts have a certain frequency, and the things that we attract to ourselves have the same frequencies as the thoughts that we have created.

For example, when we are thinking, we create brain or thought waves. Imagine that you are tuned into radio station 99.9 FM. When you are tuned into this station, you can only receive the radio waves from this station. You cannot set your radio to this station and receive the radio waves from radio station 102.1 FM. The same goes for our thinking. We cannot be thinking negative thoughts and be in harmony with positive thoughts at the same time.

Since like attracts like, you will notice that when you are tuned into positive thinking, you will attract more positive things to yourself. The same goes with negative thinking. If you start off on the wrong side of the bed in the morning and do not change your thinking, you will attract more and more negative things to you as the day progresses. It can snowball either way for you, so why not let it snowball in a positive direction?

The key is to stop your negative thinking the minute you recognize it is there. Everyone thinks negative thoughts; you just need to learn how to not think that way for a long time. Recognize it and get out of it and get on to a more productive way of thinking.

> Our thoughts travel 930,000 times faster than the sound of our voice. No other force or power in the universe yet known is as great or as quick. It is a scientifically proven fact that the mind is a battery force, the greatest of any known element.[1]
>
> *Raymond Holliwell, author of* Working with the Law

This quote is so powerful. This means that with our thoughts, we really can create anything, but we need to be on the same frequency, or wavelength, as the thing that we desire.

Our goal is to raise our vibration level. To do so, we must create two objects that are in harmony with each other. When you are not realizing a goal, it is because you and your goal are on different frequencies. Just like a radio station that you cannot hear, until you turn the dial, your goal will not materialize until you and the goal are in harmony.

---

1   Holliwell, Raymond, *Working With the Law: 11 Truths for Successful Living* (Devours and Co, 2005).

Two objects whose electromagnetic fields are the same are operating on the same frequency. Therefore, we can say they are in resonance, in harmony, or in rapport.[2]

Bob Proctor, author of You Were Born Rich

So how do you increase your level of vibration so that you can attract better things to you?

- Positive thinking will help you increase your thought waves to that higher level of vibration. Just think of how great it feels when you are driving in your car, singing your favorite song at the top of your lungs, and looking at the beauty of the landscape and nature around you. Practice recognizing how great you feel when you are looking at nature or listening to a song that makes you have great memories. When you are feeling good, you are on the right track to raising your vibration, and when you are feeling bad, you are not on the right track. Do whatever it takes to stay in that good feeling, and your vibration will continue to rise.

- Limit your activities with people who are on a lower frequency than you. You know the type: they constantly speak of what's wrong with their lives. As they complain, they are actually draining your energy. Be mindful of who you are spending time with so that you can keep your vibration up. If you hang out with someone who makes you feel bad about yourself, they can only bring you further from the good that you desire by sucking away your positive energy.

- Spend more time with like-minded people who are creative and positive like you. This will only allow you to keep increasing your vibrations. Join a club or a group in which you can meet people with interests similar to yours. Go hiking or join your local gym and notice how happy people who exercise are. It's those natural endorphins rushing through their blood that help them stay positive.

---

2   Proctor, ibid.

- Avoid watching television, especially the news, and especially before you go to sleep. I don't need to remind you of the impact that the gory news can have on your conscious mind. But remember that it only does harm to your subconscious mind. If you are really serious about raising your level of vibration, I would limit the amount of time you watch television, purely to guard the negativity from entering your mind.

- Be polite and mindful of others at all times. Over time and with practice, this will become a habit. If you are always thinking about ways to help others, it will be inevitable that your level of vibration will rise.

- Find ways that you can quiet your mind, and just spend time in this quiet. Some people use meditation, and others find great benefits from yoga. Find what works best for you to relax, and then practice quieting your mind. Be open to what might happen here, as powerful thoughts can occur to you when you quiet down and let them in.

Results of increasing your vibrations

Once you begin to increase your vibrations, you will notice that your life will become more peaceful. You won't be as quick to lash out when things are not going your way. Instead, you will think first and then respond gently.

So what does this have to do with our goals?

Because thoughts are things, they can be lined up on the same frequency as our goals where they will then be in rapport or harmony. Just like wave in water that has the same frequency as another wave in water, the two drops of water will join.

Our Thoughts Create Our Goals

Desire	Your Thought Pattern	The End Result
You want a car.	Think big. Imagine the details of the car. How does it feel to sit in the car, smell the car, drive the car? Imagine yourself driving the car.	Suddenly it becomes reality and you have the car.

Figure this out!

There are two people standing outside a car lot. One person, Mary, is looking at the red sports car, and she is thinking of all the reasons why she will never own it. She cannot afford it, and the price of gas is so high that she cannot think of how she can maintain it. And where would she put it? She doesn't have a parking space at her condo.

The second person, George, is also looking at the car lot from outside the fence. He is thinking about how he can buy the whole lot.

Which person's vibrations are in harmony with owning the car?

Some key things to note when visualizing your goals:

- Put as much detail into your vision as you can. What color is the car? What does it smell like? How do you feel while driving it?

- Do not constantly worry about your goal and whether it will become a reality. Release your worries and believe the goal will come to you. This is comparable to leaving someone a voicemail. You do not wonder if they will get the message. You know they will. So will the universe.

What do you really want to attract? Write down three things you *really* want.

1.

2.

3.

Imagine that the line below represents the wavelength of your thoughts. You are thinking thoughts that are steady, yet the amplitude, or peak of the waves, is not very high because you are really not putting much effort into your thoughts. You are the only person who can determine whether you are thinking thoughts with effort or without it.

You will attract like things to you, with this similar vibration.

Thought Pattern 1: Stable Thinking with little to no effort

An example of stable thinking with little to no effort would be a person who is thinking on autopilot. They are emitting thoughts that do not have much energy. When we *really* want something and we are not yet in harmony with that thing, we must *change* our habits to put ourselves in a new vibration. Then we will be able to attract that which we want. We need to jump to a new level of vibration.

＝ Amplitude of vibration

＝ wavelength of thought pattern

Thought Pattern 2: Use the will to focus in on what you really want

Use your will to attract that which you desire. Simply increase the amplitude of your thoughts by asking for what you want, and then believing that you will attain these things. Do not question or worry; have full belief in yourself. You must focus your goals on the screen of your mind and expect that they will come to form. Have an attitude of gratitude every day, and as each day passes you will advance steadily in the direction of your goals.

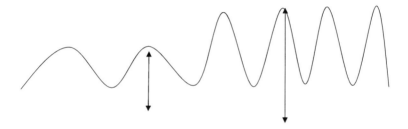

Increase the amplitude, or peak, of vibration of your thoughts by using your will.

Review

1. Single out three goals and see if you can use the will to hold the thought of having these goals on the screen of your mind.

2. Remember to have an attitude of gratitude.

3. Remember to expect your goals to materialize.

4. Do not question whether your goals are coming. Know and believe that they are on their way, and they will come.

Extension Exercise

Write about your experience. Amazing things happen when you truly believe in yourself. What happened when you really put an effort into attaining your goals?

_____

_____

_____

_____

_____

_____

_____

_____

_____

_____

_____

_____

_____

_____

_____

_____

_____

_____

_____

_____

_____

2. The Law of Polarity

The Law of Polarity states everything in the universe has an opposite. If something happens in your life that is bad, it also must contain some good. If something is a little bad, it also must be a little good. The trick is to be able to look at the good side of something, while in the midst of something bad.

Looking at the diagram below, you can see that everything just is what it is. If something is a little negative, it must also be a little positive. This law states that there is good in everything, even in bad things.

When in a negative situation, one needs to simply change one's point of view and look for something positive. Something positive will be present, but it may be difficult to see right away. Sometimes the positive aspect of a negative situation becomes evident long after the negative situation transpires. This delay usually occurs when a person has had some time to get over what upset them so much, and they are able to take a closer look at the situation.

EVERYTHING JUST IS WHAT IT IS

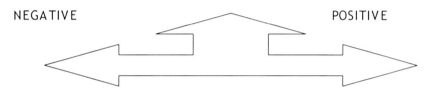

NEGATIVE   POSITIVE

Bob Proctor's *Science of Getting Rich Seminar*

Extension Exercises

1. **When something bad happens, try to see the good side. Give an example.**

   _____

   _____

   _____

   _____

2. **When you think something cannot be done and you can see fifty reasons why it cannot be done, there will also be fifty reasons why it can be done. Get into the habit of looking for possibilities instead of seeing only roadblocks to your dreams. When have you used this law?**

   _____

   _____

   _____

   _____

   _____

3. The Law of Rhythm

The Law of Rhythm states that everything is always in motion, so there will be times when we have a downswing and times when we have an upswing. No one can feel good all the time; the key is to work on maintaining even-keeled emotions.

The Law of Rhythm is Universal. This can be observed in the rising and setting of the sun and moon, ebb and flow of the tides, coming and going of the seasons, and the rhythmic swing of consciousness to unconsciousness.

Bob Proctor's SGR Seminar

POSITIVE

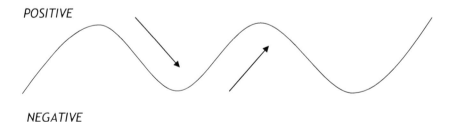

NEGATIVE

Extension Exercises

1. Know that when you are in a downswing, things can only get better. Recognize the downswing, but do not dwell in it too long. You will move on, but how long you stay there can be up to you.

2. You can still do your best, even when you are in a downswing. Doing your best will help you move faster toward an upswing.

3. Use your will to get yourself back in an upswing.

4. Give an example of a time when you were in a downswing, yet you were able to turn things around and put yourself in an upswing.

_____

_____

_____

_____

_____

_____

_____

_____

_____

_____

_____

_____

_____

_____

_____

_____

---

4. The Law of Relativity

The Law of Relativity states that all things are relative when you compare them to other things, and all things are connected. This law can be perplexing when you start to ponder, "what would you consider to be old age?" Or, "what is young?" How old would you be if you forgot your age?

This law can help increase your self-esteem if you don't think you are doing well at school, athletics, or something else that is important to you. You can always find someone else who is not doing as well as you are. Thus, it is safe to say that if you are doing the best you can, you can be proud of your accomplishments instead of being hard on yourself.

Remember that we all have different talents, and that our talents will come in handy for someone else who needs something that you can do better than they can.

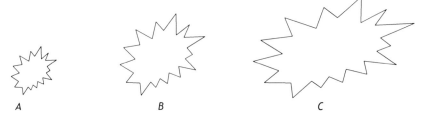

A   B   C

For example, if you are person B looking at person A, you seem bigger. And person A compared to person B looks really small. But, remember from The Law of Polarity that everything *just is what it is*. If that's the case, then A is not small, and C is not big. They just are what they are.

Extension Exercise

When something really bad happens to you, you can always find someone whose situation is much worse than your own. This makes what happened to you seem a bit more manageable. This reminds us that things are neither all good nor all bad, they just are what they are. Thus, things are not always as bad as they seem.

Explain a situation that you thought was bad, but it turned out that someone else's situation was worse than your own. The comparison allowed you to ultimately resolve your issue much faster.

_____

_____

_____

_____

_____

_____

_____

_____

5. The Law of Cause and Effect

The Law of Cause and Effect states that everything happens according to a law, and one reaction causes another, and that reaction causes another. This really is something to think about, as *every* action you take causes a ripple in the universe, and your actions change the world forever.

A good example here is with what people would know to be called karma. When you do good things, you receive good things back to you and at the same time, if you knowingly do bad things, you will attract that right back to you. It might not come from the same source (good or bad), but it will come back to you, one day.

I am sure that you have heard stories of people saying that they need to be careful of their actions, or the karma police will get them. This concept does have some truth to it, and is a good way to model your life, always being mindful of the consequences of your actions.

Everything that happens to you is a result of the thoughts you think, whether you want to believe it or not. Everything that happens to you happens for a reason. There is no such thing as chance or luck. If you do not like the results you are getting, then you will need to change the thoughts you are thinking or actions you are taking. This will afford you new conditions, circumstances, environments, and results.

Extension Exercises

1. What results would you like to change in your life?

   _____
   _____
   _____
   _____
   _____
   _____
   _____
   _____

2. Give an example of someone you know who changed his or her own life and the lives of others due to an action that person took.

   _____
   _____
   _____
   _____
   _____
   _____
   _____
   _____

6. The Law of Physical Manifestation

The Law of Physical Manifestation states that everything in the universe consists of energy, and this energy will continue to move with and through us, helping us form ideas and things.

To Understand the Unseen Part of your Conscious or Thinking Mind, Look at This!

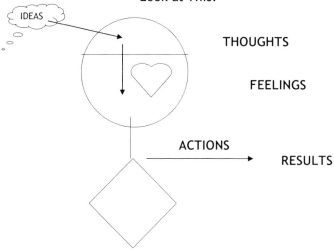

Ideas come into your conscious mind or thinking mind and create feelings. The feelings you have are expressed through the body. The body reacts to the emotions in the form of action, and results are produced.

For example, you get an idea to join the basketball team. The thought of you scoring points at home games and being the top scorer causes you to get super excited, and you fall in love with this idea. In order to make this desire a reality (making the team), you decide to practice ball every day after school. After a few months of practice, you make the team.

Extension Exercises

1. Trust the ideas that come into your mind.

2. Allow yourself to get emotionally involved with that which you want because the emotion brings your desire to you.

3. Expect that what you want will to come to you.

4. Be grateful for what you already have.

5. Act on your desire.

6. Continue to act until you attain the desired result.

7. Give an example of how you have used this law successfully.

_____

_____

_____

_____

_____

_____

Test Your Current Knowledge of Goal Setting

Now that your mind is ready and open to realize your desires, let's figure out what they are. As you move through this section, you will start to realize things about yourself you might not know. Open your mind and see what might come from this lesson. When I was first asked to write down 101 of my top goals, I had a difficult time doing so. There were probably ten goals that consumed my mind on a daily basis, but I never really thought past these. This activity helped me to really stretch and think beyond my current level of thinking. I was amazed when I wrote down that I wanted to swim with sharks. This was something I had never consciously thought about, but when asked to dig deep, this goal surfaced. I was truly amazed.

- Parents and teachers, ask yourselves, "Am I being a goal setter?" Do you know that only 1 percent of the population writes down their goals? Start now, and begin to see your dreams come into physical form.

- Teenagers and students, this is the best time in your life to be a goal setter. You have the rest of your life to bring your dreams to you. What do you really want? Dig inside your mind, and know that the first step toward goal achievement is to be clear about what you really want.

1. Do you set goals?

2. Do you know which four areas of your life you should be setting goals for?

_____

_____

_____

_____

3. Have you ever set short-term or long-term goals? If so, what happened?

_____

_____

_____

_____

4. Why is goal setting so important?

_____

_____

_____

_____

LESSON FOUR

How does goal setting and persistence set you apart from all others?

Think
About This!

- Parents and teachers, how have you been living your lives? Are you a goal achiever who's living an exciting life, or are you afraid to move toward your dreams? The first step toward living the life you desire is to write out what you really want. Maybe fear is holding you back. We will work to eliminate fears in Lesson 7. Maybe you don't think you deserve to have the life of your dreams. We will work to eliminate self-doubt in Lesson 5.

- Have you ever set a goal and wondered why it just didn't come to you? Remember The Laws of the Universe. It is time to evaluate your progress. Are you thinking positively? Are you in harmony with your goals? Do you believe and expect that they will come to you? Are you ready to do what it takes to attain them? If you are not in harmony with your goals, it may take you some time to accomplish them. If you are not achieving your goals, it just means there is more work to be done.

- Teenagers and students, as young adults with the rest of your lives ahead of you, why would you not want all of your dreams to come true? It really is simple to have the life of your dreams, but it does take time, effort, and persistence. How do you want to live your life? Let your mind soar and write down what you would like your future to look like.

A life of Mediocrity and No Fun	An Exciting Life on the Edge
These people are not goal setters.	These people are goal setters
They can make choices, but they choose not to set or attain goals.	They can make choices, and they choose to set and attain goals.
They are too busy to think creatively.	They take the time to think creatively.
They settle for a life of mediocrity and never take risks.	They experience victories, growth, happiness, satisfaction, and prosperity.
They play it safe, too afraid to make any changes.	

If you plan on being anything less than you are capable of being, you will probably be unhappy all the days of your life.

Abraham Maslow

Lesson

Goals are an incredible subject because they represent serious change in your life and improved results. Most people have no idea where to begin setting goals, so they usually never begin. Do you know that only 1 percent of the population sets goals? Most people are not willing to search deep within themselves to discover their true passions. They are too busy with their daily lives. The last thing on their minds is adding another thing to their plate.

Also, people who never set goals are safe from failure. They will also never attain any success beyond what they have in their current life. Some people actually fear success because they don't feel like they deserve it.

Finally, some people who do set goals choose goals that are not worthy of them. They settle for what they think they can accomplish, when in reality, they could strive for much greater success.

People who set goals improve the quality of their lives. People who set goals are SMART! They choose goals that are *specific*, *measurable*, *attainable*, *risky*, and *time*-specific—SMART.

Specific

Goals such as, "I want to be rich" or "I want to be happy" are not specific enough. You must choose specific goals. Here are some examples:

- I want to be attending New York State College by May 2009.

- I will reduce my weight by twenty-five pounds by June 30, 2009.

- I will go to vacation in Jamaica within the next three months.

Measurable

You must be specific with regard to numbers, time, money, and places. List exactly what you want.

Attainable

Make sure you aim high with your goals, and make sure you stretch yourself far enough. At the same time, you should set yourself up for success, without setting yourself up for failure. Your goals should both scare and excite you. This will keep you moving toward them.

Risky

If you do not stretch yourself enough and you fail to choose risky goals, you will not be living up to your ultimate potential. Be careful with whom you share your dreams. Dream stealers will tell you that you cannot do meet the goals you've set. Either keep your goals to yourself, or share them only with supportive people who will encourage you along your journey. Make your goals worthwhile, or you will never want the end result badly enough to make it through the tough times.

Time-specific

Make sure you are specific about the timeframe in which you plan to accomplish a goal. If you're not specific about a deadline, you could find yourself working toward your goal for your entire life without ever reaching your final destination.

- The goals you focus on should support your values. That way, you will stay focused on that which excites you and satisfies you the most.

- Your goals should focus on something you want, not something you need. There is only inspiration in things you want.

The Creative Process: What Do You Really Want?

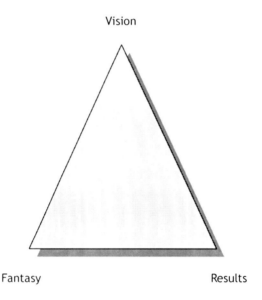

Vision

Fantasy   Results

Fantasy

Within our minds, there is a truly powerful force—our imagination. This is the first stage of creation when designing one's future. Thinking back to when you were a small child is the best way to begin to shape your future. Relax your mind and body, and take notice of what you think and feel. When you are relaxing, you are tapping into your subconscious mind.

> The imagination is literally the workshop wherein are fashioned all plans created by man.
>
> *Napoleon Hill*

When you are setting goals, you must leave your physical senses and operate through the higher faculties of your mind. Take your fantasy, create your vision, and with the right focus and determination, you will create the results you are looking for.

114

You will need to operate within The Laws of the Universe while you are working toward the formation of your goals. You will also need to hold onto your faith and purpose and maintain a willful expectation as you work toward your goals. Implementing these ideas is the perfect way to achieve a desired outcome.

It is your subconscious mind that holds you where you are. You must leave behind all competition and reach out to the creativity of your mind. Use your imagination to its fullest. Take your fantasy and create a clear mental picture on the screen of your mind. Then write it down.

Review

The First Steps to Writing Your Goals

First, think about some areas of your life where you would like to see improvement. You will want to set goals that will enrich all areas of your life so you can attain balance. What good would it do to work-out daily and have a very healthy body but have no friends? In another example, what if you spent all your time with your homework and family, but you neglected to give back to your community. Goals are all about achieving balance in these four areas of your life.

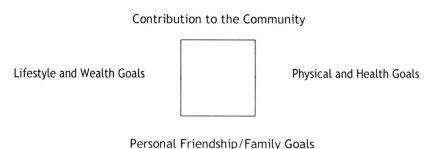

Contribution to the Community

Lifestyle and Wealth Goals   Physical and Health Goals

Personal Friendship/Family Goals

Second, choose one of the four areas and begin writing. Just let your ideas flow. I usually suggest setting 101 goals total for the four areas combined. (Choose twenty-five goals in each area). This is not an easy task. What happens is that you delve into the depths of your mind, and you pull out things you may not have been aware you were interested in. If you get stuck at fifty, keep going. Keep thinking, and your ideas will begin to flow.

Find Your Want List

List 101 things you really want, and imagine that it is impossible to fail.

Once you have written down 101 goals, prioritize them. Think of all the things you would like to accomplish in the next ninety days, in the next year, in the next three years, and in the next five years. Write either NOW, 1, 3, or 5 next to each of your goals. This determines which goals you will focus on for the next ninety days.

Now What?

Look at your list of immediate goals. Which one is most important to you? You will likely find that one of the goals will make your heart sing. You will also look at these goals and feel they are impossible to accomplish. That is normal, and that is good. Easy goals are not challenging. Find the one goal that makes you feel both uncomfortable and excited. Choose this goal to write your affirmation.

Found the Goal That Excites and Scares You?

Now, you must write an affirmation in the present tense that will assist you in visualizing your goal in physical form. You must keep your affirmation with you and recite it as often as you can. Here is an example of an affirmation of someone who wants to go to the beaches of Nantucket for vacation.

"I am so happy and grateful to be sitting on the warm sands of Madaket Beach in Nantucket on or before June 31. I can feel the sun on my skin as the wind blows my hair away from my face. I can taste the salt from the ocean on my lips. I am so thankful for the opportunity to get away for some rest and relaxation."

Another way to really get your goal engraved into your subconscious mind is to display a photograph of yourself as if you have already attained your goal. If you want a new car, then go to the car lot and take a photograph of yourself sitting in your future new car. If you want to go on vacation, find a photo of a beach and add your photo to it as if you were there.

Remember that the subconscious mind believes whatever we tell it.

Also remember that nobody is aware of what you are capable of accomplishing.

> There is a spark...within everyone, and when it is fanned into flame, it will bring forth extraordinary results.
>
> *Brandeis*

Begin to allow your imagination to flow. When you let yourself connect to your innermost thoughts, then you can begin to piece together the things you truly want. Most great goals began as fantasies on the screen of someone's mind.

Remember, there will be a hidden guide, or a dream stealer, who will attempt to knock you off course. Unfortunately, 97 percent of goal setters will give up.

You must move forward, especially during hardships.

We really can do much more than we ever give ourselves credit for.

Our habits will play mental games on us to prevent us from winning. If you can dream it, you can do it!

Extension Exercise:
My 101 Goals

1.	24.
2.	25.
3.	26.
4.	27.
5.	28.
6.	29.
7.	30.
8.	31.
9.	32.
10.	33.
11.	34.
12.	35.
13.	36.
14.	37.
15.	38.
16.	39.
17.	40.
18.	41.
19.	42.
20.	43.
21.	44.
22.	45.
23.	46.

47.	75.
48.	76.
49.	77.
50.	78.
51.	79.
52.	80.
53.	81.
54.	82.
55.	83.
56.	84.
57.	85.
58.	86.
59.	87.
60.	88.
61.	89.
62.	90.
63.	91.
64.	92.
65.	93.
66.	94.
67.	95.
68.	96.
69.	97.
70.	98.
71.	99.
72.	100.
73.	101.
74.	

Goal Tracking Sheet

Immediate Goals

1.	10.	19.
2.	11.	20.
3.	12.	21.
4.	13.	22.
5.	14.	23.
6.	15.	24.
7.	16.	25.
8.	17.	
9.	18.	

The Goal That Excites and Scares You

Notes

Test Your Current Knowledge of Persistence

Now that you have set your goals, I am sure you've met that invisible guide who seems to have been hired to knock you off course from your desires. I call this hidden guide a roadblock, and I never let him get to me. When I see Mr. Roadblock come up in the middle of my path, I find a way around him. At this point, it is important to note that you should seek out mentors to help guide you toward your destination. Find someone who has successfully attained what you are looking for and accept their advice. It will be your mentor who helps you stay on track when you want to throw in the towel.

Did you know that Art Linkletter, with no business background, interviewed twenty-seven thousand children and created the television show *Kids Say the Darnedest Things*? Do you wonder how he was able to access interviews with all these children? He went to a Los Angeles school district and looked for kids who appeared to be the smartest kid in the room. Talk about persistence.

- Parents and teachers, how have you used persistence to accomplish your goals? Think about how persistence has paid off for you.

- Teenagers and students, how have you used persistence in your life? What have you accomplished using this skill?

1. What does it mean to be persistent?

_____

_____

_____

_____

_____

2. Are you taught at school how to be persistent?

    _____

    _____

    _____

    _____

    _____

3. How do you develop persistence?

    _____

    _____

    _____

    _____

    _____

4. Do you know anyone who you think is persistent?

    _____

    _____

    _____

    _____

    _____

5. If so, how do they act, and what things do they do to make
    you think of them this way?

    _____

    _____

    _____

    _____

    _____

Think
About This!

- Parents and teachers, think about a time when you could have used persistence to attain your goals. How will you use this hindsight to help you with future goals?

- Teenagers and students, if persistence is not a part of your life yet, it is now time to think about it for your future. This one skill can land you the job of your dreams, a place in the starting lineup of the sport of your choice, and admission to the university of your choice. Being persistent takes guts, but it is a skill that everyone admires.

Lesson

Persistence is the ability to move ahead and take action regardless of how you feel about the actions you are taking. Sometimes obstacles get in our way, and they block or prevent us from taking action. But someone who is persistent will find ways to move around these obstacles and keep their eye on the end result.

Have you ever heard of life-just-happened obstacles? These are real-life issues that we must deal with. If we don't deal with them they might take us away from our goals. As much as we would like to wish these times away, they are usually intended to force us to stop and self-reflect. Sometimes serious life lessons are learned during these times. It is here that you must use The Laws of the Universe (Lesson 3) to help you stay on course.

When you are working on something, it is so easy to have motivation levels that change on a daily basis. Sometimes you feel like taking action, and other times you cannot imagine doing any work at all. Have you ever worked on a computer all day, and then at night, you just cannot imagine logging online in front of that screen? I am sure you understand this feeling. It happens to me all the time.

When you have a strong vision of your future goals, it will be impossible to give up on your dreams. You will have fleeting thoughts while driving, or you might wake up and realize you had a dream about something you really had your heart set on doing. When this happens, consider these to be signs telling you that you need to press on and take some action.

They who lack talent expect things to happen without effort. They ascribe to failure, to a lack of inspiration or ability, or to misfortune, rather than to insufficient application. At the core of every true talent, there is an awareness of the difficulties inherent in any achievement, and the confidence that by persistence and patience, something worthwhile will be realized. Thus talent is a species of vigor.

American writer Eric Hoffer (1902–1983)
was among the first to recognize the importance
of self-esteem to psychological well-being.

To bring one's self to a frame of mind and to the proper energy to accomplish things that require plain hard work continuously is the one big battle that everyone has. When this battle is won for all time, everything is easy.

Thomas A Buckner

Extension
Exercises

1. Accomplishing your goals will take vision and persistence. When have you been persistent to reach a goal? Explain.

   _____
   _____
   _____
   _____
   _____

2. There are hundreds of highly successful people. Persistence is usually the key that separates them from others. Fame comes after a very high price has been paid. Most people are not willing to pay this price. Do you know any successful people, either famous or not, who have paid a huge price to get to where they are? If so, explain their successes.

   _____
   _____
   _____
   _____
   _____
   _____

3. Skills, schooling, and personality will not give you persistence. Why do you think this is the case?

   _____
   _____
   _____
   _____
   _____
   _____

4. Persistence goes hand in hand with determination. What is determination, and when have you used it?

_____

_____

_____

_____

_____

_____

_____

5. How can you become persistent? No one can develop this skill for you. It must become a way of your life. You must want something first, then fall in love with the idea of having that thing, and persistence will follow. You must decide what you really want. Do you know what you want?

_____

_____

_____

_____

_____

_____

_____

6. Are you prepared to trade your life as you know it for your goal? This is what it will take to bring your goal into physical form.

_____

_____

_____

_____

_____

_____

7. Listen to the whispers within your heart. They give you messages that tell you why you need to be doing certain things. There is a power or energy that flows through us that gives us messages; this energy tells us what we should be doing with our lives. Listen to what you feel. You are worthy of the things you want. What whispers are in your heart?

_____

_____

_____

_____

_____

_____

_____

_____

_____

_____

_____

_____

_____

_____

When your want or desire is weak, you will quit at the first obstacle. When the dream is big enough, nothing else matters. Your dream needs to be nursed until it comes alive; then that dream will bring you alive. Have you decided what you really want? If not, problems or obstacles in your life will always defeat you and give you reasons to procrastinate. When the dream is big enough, nothing else matters.

8. Write out your dream. Remember, most dreams begin on the screen of your mind. They take physical form when you create them.

_____

_____

_____

_____

_____

_____

_____

Test Your Current Knowledge of Confidence

Now that you are moving in the direction of your goals and you have used persistence to bypass all the roadblocks, you are on the threshold of a whole new life. You will be facing new conditions and circumstances and a whole new environment, and you will definitely need to have confidence while on your journey. Do not be afraid to take risks, and do not be afraid to fail. You must take action.

- Parents and teachers, do you think your self-confidence is high? Think about how being confident in certain situations helped you to advance in your life.

- Teenagers and students, are there times when you know you are not being as confident as you know you could be? Use this lesson to help create a confidence formula that will assist you in staying calm and centered, even under pressure.

1. What does the word confidence mean to you?

_____

_____

_____

_____

_____

2. Do you think you are confident? Why or why not?

_____

_____

_____

_____

_____

3. How important do you think confidence is in your daily life and in achieving results?

_____
_____
_____
_____
_____

4. Do you believe your inner thoughts can be seen on your body or face?

_____
_____
_____
_____
_____

5. How does your confidence affect your results?

_____
_____
_____
_____
_____

6. What is the difference between someone who is confident and someone who is arrogant?

_____
_____
_____
_____
_____

7. Can someone else affect your level of confidence? Why or why not?

_____
_____
_____
_____
_____

8. Can your confidence affect your world around you? If so, how? If not, why not?

_____

_____

_____

_____

_____

9. What are some qualities of someone who has confidence?

_____

_____

_____

_____

_____

10. What does self-esteem have to do with confidence?

_____

_____

_____

_____

_____

How can the confidence formula and body image give you predictable results for success?

Think
About This!

- Parents and teachers, do you think that being confident has helped you attain your goals in life? Do you have any regrets with your life and wish you had honed this skill better? You can have confidence. Did you know that many successful people have struggled with their confidence levels? One speaker I met back in the year 2000, had become highly successful in the restaurant business, but there was a time when he could not read. He suggested that once you find something to do that you love, you will become highly successful as you specialize in this area where your heart sings. Once you have found this joy, you can always work on areas of weakness that will help you grow to a higher level of success.

- Teenagers and students, are you confident in all areas of your life? Take a close look at these exercises to see how you can further improve your self-confidence and the results you attain.

Lesson

What is Confidence?

Have you ever noticed someone who walked into a room and seemed to catch everyone's attention? They carry with them some sort of style or charisma that you notice, and so does everyone else. This is confidence. When we know that we can handle any challenge that comes our way, and we become better risk-takers, we have found confidence. People who have confidence know they can solve whatever problem they face. These people know that they are never alone. They know that they will always have all the help they need with whatever challenges they come across. When these people have a deep desire to do something, they just do it. If you doubt or question yourself and your abilities, you will never move forward toward your goals.

How Can We Develop Confidence?

We already have confidence. It's that feeling you get when you "just know" an answer. When you "just know" something, and a challenge occurs, it is easier to overcome that challenge. The hard part is listening to that feeling and not questioning whether it is right or wrong. Listen to it, and make a decision to act on it, immediately.

Confidence comes when you understand who you are as a person. An unhappy person usually gets angry or irritated easily. The cause of their problem is that they lack of self-confidence. Self-confidence produces a calmness or peacefulness within a person. These people know the answers, and they do not feel the need to brag about it. Braggers lack self-confidence. Bragging makes a bragger feel better. There is a fine line between having an air of confidence and being conceited. When you are conceited, you know you are good, and people find you arrogant. Confidence is found in people who know they are good but attribute their success to something that comes from deep within themselves. Your confidence will keep you going when you get rejected.

Remember that your body is a physical picture of what is happening in your mind. If you are unhappy, it will show on your whole body. Similarly, if you are happy, this will be obvious to everyone. All we ever need to be happy is to be aware of who we are. Many very nice people in the world have no confidence. There are also many people who are in abusive relationships who have no confidence to stand up to another person and make some changes.

Some people also stay in very boring jobs because they do not have the confidence to step out and try something new. Others let people take advantage of them because they are afraid to speak up.

Review

Confidence Check

To check your confidence, see what your self-image is like. What picture comes to your mind when you think of yourself? Do you see yourself as a powerful, wonderful human being with infinite potential? Or do you see others as being better than you? Do you constantly downplay what you are good at? Or do you know deep within that you are on track. If the latter is the case, you never feel the need to get confirmation from someone else that you are okay. If you constantly need approval or the opinion of others, you are obviously not confident in yourself. If others notice things about you that you cannot see, you need to further develop your confidence. If you have a positive self-image, chances are you are a confident person.

1. Write a paragraph that explains what you think of yourself. Be honest.

_____

_____

_____

_____

_____

_____

_____

_____

_____

_____

_____

_____

_____

_____

2. What did you learn about yourself?

_____

_____

_____

_____

_____

_____

_____

_____

_____

_____

_____

_____

_____

3. In what area do you see the need for the most improvement?

_____

_____

_____

_____

_____

_____

_____

_____

_____

_____

_____

_____

_____

Confidence also has to do with faith. How much faith do you have in yourself? You must be open to new ideas and be willing to challenge the beliefs that you already have. Beliefs cause us to make choices that may prevent us from achieving our goals. Do you have faith in yourself? Do you trust that you will be a success in whatever task you choose to tackle?

Train yourself to always see the good in other people as well. What you think of others is a reflection of what you think of yourself. Love people and let them know they are loved, and you in turn will be loved, and your confidence will soar.

4. **Think of and explain a time when you felt really confident.**

_____

_____

_____

_____

_____

_____

_____

5. **Think of and explain a time when you felt less than confident.**

_____

_____

_____

_____

_____

_____

_____

6. **Think of all the things you have refrained from doing because you lacked confidence. Free yourself from these chains and create a powerful affirmation for the things you _really_ want.**

_____

_____

_____

_____

_____

_____

_____

_____

_____

_____

_____

Extension
Exercises

The Confidence Formula

Write an affirmation in the box below. Focus on where you'd like to see yourself in the near future. Write it in the present tense so you begin to live your affirmation now. I am so happy and grateful that...

See yourself as the powerful being you are and visualize this statement three times a day.

Then, you must act so you can bring what you desire toward you. You will have a written image of the new you. When you read it, you will feel good.

If a negative thought creeps into your mind, remember to say "stop!" My affirmation contains words like power, energy, security, tranquility, peace, success, happiness, health, and wealth. I say these words *every* time I doubt myself and sometimes I just repeat these words in my head when I am exercising to give my day an energy boost. At times it is hard to get my mind off the negative path, but as soon as I say these words, my body relaxes, and I again feel at ease.

Write Your Affirmation Here:

1. **Do you know of any celebrities who used affirmations or the power of their mind to attain his or her goals?**

_____

_____

_____

_____

_____

_____

_____

_____

_____

_____

_____

_____

_____

What Does Success Mean To You?

Remember never to compare yourself to others. Create your own definition of what success means to you because success is the progressive realization of something that is important to you. Success will come to you with time; it will not come instantly. It comes with intense focus. Write out all the things success means to you. Then, remind yourself of your value, and never emphasize your mistakes. Your success is up to you.

Use Your Confidence to Calmly Deal with Difficult People

There are times when using your confidence will come into play. When dealing with someone who is difficult, your attitude is important. Maintain your balance and stay centered. Stay focused on the outcome of the situation so you can reach a conclusion without first having an argument. Always remember to speak with the proper tone of voice, a tone that is not argumentative.

Everything that happens to you is in direct relation to how you see yourself.

What Do You Expect for Yourself?

Our lives are shaped by our expectations. Things you want, and that which you expect, will come to you. What you think you cannot have will not come to you. If we believe there is no solution to a problem, we will never see the solution. Sometimes it is fear that holds us back; sometimes we are held back by the fact that we don't know what we really want. This program will assist you in figuring out exactly what you want. It will then teach you to expect to receive all the good life has to offer.

Review

1. In which areas of your life would you like to be more confident?

_____

_____

_____

_____

2. What are the next action steps you need to take in order to develop your confidence?

_____

_____

_____

_____

3. What does success mean to you?

_____

_____

_____

_____

4. How will your life look if you further develop your confidence?

_____

_____

_____

_____

_____

Extension
Exercise

Take the affirmation you created and write it somewhere where you can easily see it. Use an erasable marker on your mirror or write on a piece of paper and hang it on your wall. Repeat this affirmation three times a day and be prepared to explain what happens. How do you feel when you are saying the statement? Do you really believe it?

_____

_____

_____

_____

_____

_____

_____

_____

_____

_____

Test Your Current Knowledge
of Responsibility

As you move toward your goals, you will need to take this new life seriously. In order to continue to advance in life, you will need to continue to show a high level of responsibility. This means that you must be responsible for your actions.

- Parents and teachers, think about how important being responsible has been in your life. Think of the many instances when you have been faced with the decision to do the right thing or not.

- Teenagers and students, this chapter will show you the importance of being a responsible citizen. If you can be trusted by those around you, you will certainly advance toward your goals.

1. What does responsibility mean to you?

_____
_____
_____
_____
_____
_____

2. Do you think you are responsible? Why, or why not?

_____
_____
_____
_____
_____

3. How important do you think responsibility is in your daily life and to your results? Give one example.

_____

_____

_____

_____

_____

_____

_____

_____

_____

4. What are you responsible for?

_____

_____

_____

_____

_____

_____

5. How does it make you feel when someone says, "I know you can do that job?"

_____

_____

_____

_____

_____

6. What careers require a lot of responsibility?

_____

_____

_____

_____

_____

_____

_____

7. Think of someone you know who is responsible. What characteristics do they have?

_____

_____

_____

_____

_____

_____

_____

8. Have you ever let someone down who was counting on you to be responsible? How did you feel? How could you make the situation better?

_____

_____

_____

_____

_____

_____

_____

9. What does it mean to be responsible for your thoughts?

_____

_____

_____

_____

_____

_____

10. How could you be more responsible?

_____

_____

_____

_____

_____

_____

LESSON SIX

Why will responsibility shape your future?

Think
About This!

- Parents and teachers, think about your talents and abilities. Are you continuing to develop them?

- Teenagers and students, this lesson is just as important as the lesson about attitude. Taking responsibility for your actions is one of the most important lessons in this program.

Are you aware that some people in prisons have more freedom than others? Responsibility is your key to freedom.[1]

Viktor Frankl (1905–1997), Holocaust survivor and author of Man's Search for Meaning, *which outlines his experiences as a concentration camp inmate during World War II.*

---

1 Frankl, Viktor, *Man's Search for Meaning*, (Boston, MA: Beacon Press, 2006).

Lesson: How Responsible Decisions Will Affect Your Life

The decisions you make throughout your life will determine how you will think, feel, and act. Your life must have meaning; if it didn't, you will walk about like a zombie with no sense of purpose or vision of the future. You would be bored, and you'd feel that you did not have a purpose on this place called Earth.

On the other hand, a person can decide that they will be a winner by taking responsibility for their life. Responsible people decide what they want; then they set out immediately to find a way to realize their greatest desire. They are aware that they will face many roadblocks along the way, but the obstacles faced do not hold them back. The obstacles catapult these winners forward with more enthusiasm and energy than they had when they started.

1. What gives your life meaning or purpose? What makes you wake up and get out of bed with enthusiasm?

    _____
    _____
    _____
    _____
    _____

2. Do you know that you have special talents and abilities that no one else on the planet possesses?

    _____
    _____
    _____
    _____

3. What have you done to develop your talents and abilities?

_____

_____

_____

_____

_____

What does it mean to be a responsible person?

Read and write what you think of each statement below. Do you agree/disagree? Explain why.

1. Responsible people know exactly what they want out of life, relationships, and their lifestyle.

_____

_____

_____

_____

2. Responsible people set out immediately to get what they want.

_____

_____

_____

_____

3. Responsible people face roadblocks head on without getting intimidated by challenges.

_____

_____

_____

_____

4. Responsible people use challenges as a way to improve themselves and reach a greater height.

_____

_____

_____

_____

5. Responsible people spend their time wisely, always thinking of ways to improve their current situation.

_____

_____

_____

_____

_____

6. Responsible people are very careful with the thoughts they think and the people they surround themselves with.

_____

_____

_____

_____

7. Responsible people choose positive thoughts and work to eliminate negative thoughts by shouting out "switch" when a negative thought creeps into their mind.

_____

_____

_____

_____

_____

8. Responsible people know that their thoughts determine their feelings. They also know that this determines their final results.

_____

_____

_____

_____

9. Responsible people just do it—they take action now.

_____

_____

_____

_____

_____

10. Responsible people never blame others for their failures.

_____

_____

_____

_____

11. Responsible people use their will to hold certain positive thoughts on the screen of their mind.

_____

_____

_____

_____

12. Responsible people understand that resentment is a waste of energy.

_____

_____

_____

_____

Responsible Decision-Making Celebrities

Think of someone famous you've heard of who worked his or her way to the top. Do you know the history of the following artists/celebrities?

Jim Carrey

Google Jim Carrey to learn more about the history of this Canadian celebrity who hit it big in Hollywood after he followed his heart to Los Angeles.

Did you know that Jim Carrey started his career by performing at the well-known Toronto comedy club Yuk Yuks? [1] If only I were a few years older, I could have been watching him as a young student in Toronto who visited this local comedy club with my high school friends. Imagine that!

1 Hamilton Spectator Interview (February 2007)

155

After performing on the comedy circuit for a few years, he packed all of his belongings and moved to Los Angeles to begin his film career and became a tremendous success.

Some would say, "Oh, he is just lucky!" Others would say, "Oh, I could never do what he has done."

If I were to meet Jim Carrey, I would want to find out what made him move from Hamilton, Ontario, what stopped him from working at the Dofasco Steel Mill, and what brought him to the result of earning twenty million dollars a movie in the United States. He really must have been following his inner guidance, and he must have had great mentors and incredible belief in himself to embrace his talents to this degree. I am sure Carrey would have a lot to tell me about his path to fame.

Mary J. Blige

Google Mary J. Blige to learn more about the history of the Queen of Hip-Hop and Soul. Why is she a role model?

Did you know that, according to Wikipedia, "this African-American R&B soul, and hip hop soul singer-songwriter, occasional rapper, record producer, actress, and hip hop icon who has sold more than 40 million albums worldwide"? How did she get to this point?[2]

She lived in Yonkers, New York, and dropped out of high school her junior year. Instead of wasting her time and talents, she recorded herself singing Anita Baker's "Caught up in the Rapture" on a karaoke machine at a mall in White Plains, New York.

Blige's stepfather passed the tape to Uptown Records CEO Andre Harrell,[3] who was impressed with Blige's voice and signed her to sing backup for local acts like Father MC. Her career began. Again, some would say "Oh, she is just lucky." If I were ever to meet up with Mary J. Blige, I would ask her if she envisioned the success ahead of

2   Wilkopedia, The Free Encyclopedia.
3   Mary J. Blige Biography on Starpulse.com

her when she walked through that mall in White Plains, New York. I have been to White Plains, and it's amazing to imagine that this place is where Mary J. Blige started such a successful career.

People who accept responsibility make certain that the time they invest in a project is put to good use. They make sure they spend their time wisely, because they know that time is money. They would never be involved in activities that would waste their time. They travel the world, meet other interesting people with whom they have lots in common, and expand their minds to new experiences.

Some people may look at this type of person and say "Wow, that guy is so lucky. He leads such a rich and exciting life." The truth of the matter is that the man in question has earned the right to all the good he has brought into his life.

If something happens that attempts to knock one of these people off their feet, a responsible person faces the challenge head on. There is no pouting, whining, or saying, "Why does this always happen to me?" The challenge is looked at as a way to improve and reach greater heights.

What Are the First Steps to Taking Responsibility?

When you take responsibility for yourself, you begin by taking responsibility for your thoughts. Thinking is the first step toward changing your results. You must first think something; then your thoughts cause the actions that in turn cause results.

What thoughts do you have? Do you sometimes think negative thoughts such as "I could never do that?" Don't forget that what you think determines the results you achieve, so it is very important to be careful what you think about. Being responsible begins with choosing responsible thoughts.

When people reject responsibility, they turn their lives over to others in hope that something good will happen. We know that the only way to achieve results in our lives is to just do it. We know that no one else will realize these results for you. They are too worried about the things they wish they were doing.

Responsible People Never Blame Others for Their Results

> People are always blaming their circumstances for what they are.
>
> *George Bernard Shaw (1856–1950), the only person to have been awarded both a Nobel Prize for literature, which he won in 1925, and an Oscar, which he won in 1938 for the film Pygmalion.*

Have you ever blamed someone for something that happened to you that you did not like? Give an example of what happened and how you felt.

_____

_____

_____

_____

_____

_____

The blame game is a dumb game. Blaming does not change what happened. When you blame others for the results you achieve, you are not being responsible.

When you take responsibility for yourself, you understand that you are responsible for your thoughts, feelings, actions, and all the results you create in your life. You realize when something goes wrong in your life that you brought the situation on yourself. No one did it to you.

When you understand this crucial aspect of responsibility, we can eliminate blaming others for out downfalls. In turn, we face up to the challenges we create in our own lives. In addition, we also know that when good things happen in our lives, we are responsible for those as well.

I choose my thoughts, and I therefore choose the conditions, circumstances, and environment that I attract into my life. I know that everything I have in my life is a direct result of the thoughts I have been thinking.

What Makes You So Special?

I am special because I have the ability to think. This is what separates me from the animal kingdom. In this whole universe, there is only one me. There has never been, nor will there ever be, another me. I am a unique child of the universe. I can think and use my will to hold certain thoughts in my mind. I can think about getting good grades, making the track team, and eating lunch with my best friends. Or I can think about how poorly I think I will do on my math test, that the coach will probably cut me from the track team, or that no one will eat lunch with me. It is up to each individual to decide which thoughts he or she chooses to put into their mind. Whatever you think about, you attract into your life. Therefore, you might as well choose the positive thought over thoughts of lack and limitation.

Do Wasted Emotions Zap Your Energy?

Along with blame, you must also understand that resentment can only hurt you. It is a wasted emotion. You can exert your energy much more productively if you refrain from wasting it on a bad emotion. You know not to blame others for your results and you must also get rid of any resentment you have in your life. You must take 100 percent responsibility for every action in your life without blaming others or being resentful when things do not go your way.

Remember that you are responsible for:

- Your life

- Your feelings

- Your learning and growth

- Your results

Review

1. In which areas of your life do you want to become more responsible?

_____

_____

_____

_____

_____

_____

_____

_____

_____

_____

2. Write out the action steps you will take to improve responsibility in your life.

_____

_____

_____

_____

_____

_____

_____

_____

_____

_____

_____

3. When have you blamed someone for your results? How will you prevent yourself from blaming others in the future?

_____

_____

_____

_____

_____

_____

_____

_____

_____

4. When have you been resentful? How will you prevent yourself from wasting your energy on this emotion in the future?

_____

_____

_____

_____

_____

_____

_____

_____

5. How will your life change when you begin to take complete responsibility for it?

_____

_____

_____

_____

_____

_____

_____

Extension
Exercises

Pick something that would require responsibility to accomplish. Be prepared to explain your level of commitment to the task and whether you took complete responsibility for its attainment. How did you do? How did you feel? Did you receive praise for your commitment?

Test Your Current Knowledge of Your Habits and Beliefs

You have been working diligently with this program, doing the activities, paying attention to your thinking, and yet you seem to be getting nowhere. Instead of giving up, take a closer look at some of your habits and beliefs. In order to attain change in your life, you may need to change some habits. This is the hardest work in the world because you have become used to doing things a certain way. How badly do you want change to occur in your life? If you are serious about a new life, then you will endure the uncomfortable stages as you make changes and break some of the habits that might be holding you back without your knowledge. Changing your life just a little now will make a massive difference to your future.

- Parents and teachers, in this chapter you will focus on the things that hold you back. You might have some habits or ways of living that you are accustomed to. These paradigms may be preventing you from attaining something you really want. What is holding you back from going after the things you really want in life?

- Teenagers and students, because you are still young, changing habits that do not work for you will be much easier than it will be for adults who have done things the same way for years. You are at an advantage here, so be sure to make use of the fact that you can make changes in this area. Think about the things you would really like to do, and discover if there is anything holding you back.

1. What holds you back from doing the things you really want to do?

_____

_____

_____

_____

_____

_____

_____

2. Are you aware that you have habits or programs that prohibit you from achieving your greatest potential?

_____

_____

_____

_____

_____

_____

_____

3. Where do you think your beliefs came from?

_____

_____

_____

_____

_____

_____

_____

4. Have you ever challenged any of the beliefs you hold? If so, which ones?

_____

_____

_____

_____

_____

_____

_____

5. When do you feel fear, and what happens to you in this situation?

_____

_____

_____

_____

_____

_____

_____

6. Does fear stop you from accomplishing great things?

_____

_____

_____

_____

_____

_____

_____

7. Has anything from your past prevented you from moving forward?

_____

_____

_____

_____

_____

8. Have you ever taken charge and noticed incredible things happening? When were they?

_____

_____

_____

_____

_____

_____

_____

9. When have you ever doubted your abilities so much that you felt sick to your stomach with worry?

_____

_____

_____

_____

_____

_____

_____

_____

_____

_____

10. Is there something you really want but are too afraid to go after?

_____

_____

_____

_____

_____

_____

_____

_____

LESSON SEVEN

How can you turn your life around by blasting through things that make you nervous?

Think
About This!

To ignore the power of your paradigms to influence your judgment is to put yourself at significant risk when exploring the future. To be able to shape your future, you must be ready and able to change your paradigm.

Joel Barker, futurist and author of Paradigms:
Business of Discovering the Future, published in 1992.
He was the first person to speak about paradigm shifts
in the corporate world.

Prepare

- Parents and teachers, think about things that hold you back and determine how they have changed the course of your life. How would your life be different if you had never let those things hold you back? What are you willing to do to blast though those habits that are no longer serving you? How badly do you want to see change in your life?

- Teenagers and students, you are so lucky that you have your whole life ahead of you. If there are things that are holding you back, then you have many years to work on them. You have it much easier than adults who have years of habits ingrained in their minds. Keep your eyes on your goal, and move past all that could be holding you back.

Lesson

What is a Paradigm? Do I Have One?

Culture is known to have been founded on habits, attitudes, beliefs, and expectations. These beliefs are called paradigms. When you are able to change your paradigms, you are able to challenge the beliefs you have formed. Then you can look at the world with different pair of eyes.

> People do not resist change when it is their choice. People resist being changed.
>
> *Michael Basch, FedEx cofounder*

Some paradigms you have are really just other people's habits. Some people believe that it would be absolutely horrible to eat sheep intestines, yet the Scottish eat Haggis and love it. Can you think of other examples like this one where the beliefs that other people have are not the same as your own?

Where Did Your Paradigms Come From?

How did you form your current set of beliefs? They were likely derived from your parents, friends, teachers, and so on. But where did those people get their beliefs? They probably derived them from their own parents, friends, teachers, and so on. So, who is to say that the beliefs we have are 100 percent accurate? We must be open to challenging what we already know, or what we think we know.

Working With Your Beliefs or Paradigms

We are programmed genetically (from your parents and their parents) as well as environmentally. Where we live determines many of the belief systems we will form. If we want to experience *new* things, we must be ready to challenge some of the limiting beliefs we have that hold us back and keep us from accomplishing the great things we know we are capable of. We must really take a good look at the things we believe. Is our behavior in line with our beliefs? Are our thoughts, feelings, and actions all lined up? If so, you are in integrity with yourself.

If you *believe* you can do something, you must step out and do it, regardless of the things that are holding you back.

Changing Your Paradigms

Successful people do well what others feel uncomfortable doing.

We must keep in mind that we have a powerful energy flowing through us and that all things are possible when we learn to use all of our higher faculties—intuition, reason, the will, creativity, imagination, perception, and memory—instead of just living through our five senses.

What Results Will I Achieve?

Changing just a few paradigms or habits can make an enormous difference in your life. If you have a hard time speaking in front of other people, imagine how your life would change if you began to speak fluently in front of large audiences. If you always thought you were not good enough to sing in public, imagine how your life would change if you got the role in the school play with the singing part.

Remember there will be no change in your life until the paradigm has been changed. To change the paradigm, you must learn to go through the terror barrier.

Review

1. Choose two things you would really love to do but you are too afraid to do. Write them down, and create an affirmation explaining that you are so happy and grateful now that you have accomplished these two things.

_____
_____
_____
_____
_____
_____

2. Write down five action steps that you will implement in an effort to accomplish these two things.

_____
_____
_____
_____
_____
_____

3. What old habits or paradigms came up when you attempted to accomplish the two things? How did you overcome these paradigms?

_____
_____
_____
_____
_____
_____

4. **What does Mary Anne Williamson say in the following passage? (Bonus points if you can name the movie that this passage was read in.)**

Our worst fear is not that we are inadequate; our deepest fear is that we are powerful beyond measure. It is our light, not our darkness that most frightens us. We ask ourselves, who am I to be brilliant, gorgeous, talented, and fabulous. Actually, who are you not to be ... your playing small does not serve the world. There is nothing enlightened about shrinking so that other people won't feel insecure around you ... As we let our own light shine, we unconsciously give other people permission to do the same. As we are liberated from our own fear, our presence automatically liberates others.

Mary Ann Williamson. Used by Nelson
Mandela in his 1994 inaugural speech

_____
_____
_____
_____
_____
_____

Extension
Exercise

Think of one of the two things that you want to do, but you're too scared to do. Step through the terror barrier, and take your first steps toward accomplishing something very scary. Be prepared to explain what you did and how it felt.

Lesson

The Change Mechanism: Let Go Of the Past for a Brighter Future

To break through the Change Mechanism, you must be ready to let go of the past. Whenever there is a major shift in your life, you find yourself face-to-face with the Change Mechanism. When you are making a decision and you start to feel scared deep inside the pit of your stomach, you have hit the Change Mechanism. Your *entire* central nervous system goes off as you think of a *new* thought in your conscious mind.

> You will either step forward into *growth*, or you will step back into *safety*.
>
> *Abraham Harold Maslow (1908–1970),*
> *American psychologist noted for his concept of*
> *the hierarchy of human needs. He is also*
> *considered the father of humanistic psychology.*

Help, I am Stuck!

In this situation, the person is totally living in their comfort zone. Life is easy, because they are not stretching outside the box. There is no discomfort or fear. However, this person is living a life of mediocrity. He or she could be capable of so much more, but they are afraid to venture out of their old paradigms. It is a person's subconscious mind that keeps them where there are with their current results.

1. Write about a time you felt this happened to you.

_____

_____

_____

_____

_____

_____

_____

_____

_____

_____

_____

_____

_____

_____

_____

_____

_____

_____

_____

_____

_____

Ahhh! I Am Frustrated!

In this situation, a person starts to see other people achieving their own goals and desires, and they start to want their own new experiences. Desire starts to poke through and push this person to make a change. Often, the first feeling is frustration because the person finds himself in an unsatisfying situation, but this is usually what motivates the person to make a change.

2. When have you been motivated to make a change in your life?

_____
_____
_____
_____
_____
_____
_____
_____
_____

I am making changes, but I feel so uncomfortable!

In this situation, a person decides that it is time to make a change and step toward their desires. Maybe the person wants to buy a new car, or move to a new state. Suddenly, in the middle of the decision-making process, they feel as if their entire central nervous system has gone out of control, and they are overcome with fear. They think they have made a mistake, and they start to question their decisions. What you need to do when you are here is move forward, and do not look back.

3. Describe a time when you were in this situation.

_____
_____
_____
_____
_____
_____
_____
_____
_____

Break Free of Your Past

Freedom

This is the step that is achieved when a person steps out of his or her comfort zone, feels uncomfortable, but does it anyway and keeps moving toward growth.

There is nothing like experiencing the feeling of hitting your target, when you have had your eye on a goal for a very long time. It feels great!

4. **Write about a time you hit a goal after focusing with all your efforts to achieve it.**

_____

_____

_____

_____

_____

_____

_____

_____

_____

_____

Test Your Current Knowledge of Self-Motivation, Values, Integrity, and Self-Image

Say that you have been working on these exercises, getting rid of all those habits that have been holding you back from attaining your goals, yet the results are still are not forthcoming. You are about ready to throw this book out, and then you realize there is still more that could be holding you back. This section will show you the power of being self-motivated when times are difficult. Also, if you are out of line with your values and integrity, it will not be possible to advance. Finally, your self-image is the key to your goal attainment. If you are out of line with any of these, you must go back to the drawing board and do some more work.

> When you are doing something with your life, you will get
> problems. Problems are a sign that you are doing something.
> *Doug Wead, an author, humanitarian,*
> *and philanthropist, who has written twenty-seven*
> *books that have cumulatively sold five million copies*
> *and have been translated into thirty languages*

- Parents and teachers, in this lesson, think about your core values. Consider whether you think you live in line with these values.

- Teenagers and students, this lesson is built around the values that you think are most important to you. Think about these things and your self-image while reading this chapter. When you have a strong self-image, you should be able to stay in integrity with your values.

1. Why must you be self-motivated to reach any level of success in your life?

    _____
    _____
    _____
    _____
    _____
    _____

2. What values are important to you?

    _____
    _____
    _____
    _____
    _____

3. Are you in line with your values? Why or why not?

    _____
    _____
    _____
    _____
    _____

4. What does body image have to do with self-motivation, your values, and integrity?

    _____
    _____
    _____
    _____
    _____

LESSON EIGHT

How do self-motivation and your values help you live a decent life of integrity?

Think
About This!

- Parents and teachers, we are nearing the last lesson in this book, so I must ask, "Are you still are having some challenges attaining your goals?"

If you really are doing everything correctly, then sometimes you will have to stop and think that the goal that you want might not be right for you at this specific time. All goals have an incubation period. It's not easy to predict when that incubation period will end, but you must have faith that you will see your desired results. One of my goals took three years to fulfill. Another took twelve years. If you really want to achieve a particular goal, you will be patient and continue to take action steps toward it. You will need to be honest about your level of motivation and whether or not you are living in line with your values. Also, your self-image is important for the attainment of your goals. If you do not think you are deserving of your goal, and you are the only one who really knows this, then you will have some issues with goal attainment. Once all of these concepts line up, you will be well on your way to living the life of your dreams.

- Teenagers and students, are you self-motivated? Can you give up something of a lower nature to receive something of a higher nature?

For example, are you capable of staying home on a Friday night and not going out with your friends in order to study so you will receive an A on a paper? Are you willing to pay the price of success? Do you know what values are important in your life, and do you live in line with these values? Do you have a positive self-image? Do you think other people respect you?

Lesson

What is Self-Motivation?

To be successful, you must make things happen. You must be self-motivated. Self-motivation is the force that takes your desire and lets it drive you to achieve your goals. This does not come easy for everyone. This process is how high achievers bridge the gap between thinking about their goals and actually accomplishing them.

> Man is ultimately self-determining. Man does not simply exist but always decides what his existence will be, what he will become in the next moment. By the same token, every human being has the freedom to change at any instant.
> *Holocaust survivor, neurologist and psychiatrist*
> *Viktor Frankl in* Man's Search for Meaning

How Do You Become Self-Motivated?

- You must believe in yourself. You must honor who you are and know that you are worthy and deserve to achieve your goals.

- You must love to be challenged, be flexible when change occurs, set outstanding goals, and be proud of your success.

- You must be able to overcome fear. The best way to do this is to continue working despite your fear.

- Be bold and begin now.

Seize this very minute; what you can do, or dream you can do, begin it! Boldness has genius, power and magic in it; only engage and the mind grows heated; begin at once and the work will be completed.

Johann von Goethe (1749–1832), author of
great literary works including poetry, drama,
literature, theology, humanism and science.

Self-motivated people know that they must take the lead and begin the project. Nothing happens until something is begun.

They also know that they must be the ones to follow through and finish the project. Focus on the result. Think of how good it will feel when you finally achieve your goal. You must have a clear mental picture of what the end result will look like. You will be motivated when you think of this image.

Discovering Your Identity to Help You Move Forward

Before you can venture into your future, you must first know who you are so you can guide yourself toward your success. Who are you? What is important to you? Have you ever ended a relationship and felt you lost your identity? It is very important at these times that you step back and really take the time to get to know yourself. Only by solidly understanding of who you are can you ever progress toward your goals. Finding another relationship to fill the void is not the best solution. You will only find unhappiness, as you can never expect another person to make you happy—that is your job.

You must also learn to see yourself as others see you so that you can make corrections or changes if you need to. Feedback from others is sometimes very difficult to hear, but if you are serious about your growth, you will accept it graciously. It is not easy to be honest with yourself and open up to the truth of exactly who you are and how you are perceived by others. You must look at your attitude and self-image, and you must also look at how you treat other people and any limiting beliefs you have that may be preventing you from attaining your goals.

If you have a friend you trust, ask him or her what he or she thinks of you as a friend. If you have children, ask them how you are doing as a parent. I learned a lot about how others saw me from attending an eye-opening seminar series called *PSI Seminars* in Clearlake Oaks, California. The feedback I received at these seminars was enough for me to clearly see why I was not progressing toward my goals.

Are You in Integrity with Your Values?

You must be in integrity with your values. You can learn what your values are when you look at your thoughts, feelings, and actions and consider what is most important to you. If you are not listening to the values that are of utmost importance to you, then you will always have a difficult time attaining your goals.

To discover what your values are, answer these questions about things you think, feel, and act on.

1. What is my attitude toward other people?

   _____

   _____

   _____

   _____

   _____

2. What moral issues are important to me?

   _____

   _____

   _____

   _____

   _____

3. How do I want to be seen by my friends, family, and community?

   _____

   _____

   _____

   _____

4. **What values do I want those close to me to have?**

_____

_____

_____

_____

_____

5. **How do I want other people to treat me?**

_____

_____

_____

_____

_____

Once you know what your values are, you can set your goals in the proper priority. Then you must make sure that you stay true to your values. It does you no good to value truth, for example, but not be able to speak your own truths as you work to achieve your goals.

For example, imagine that telling the truth is important to you, and someone asks you something about yourself that you are not comfortable speaking about. Maybe you are shy and do not want to brag about the lofty goals that you have set for yourself. If you value telling the truth, you really should open up and answer that person's question so that you can remain in integrity with all that is important to you.

Another example of being in integrity happens when I tell someone that I am going to the gym. Now, exercising is important to me, and so is telling the truth. So, if I decide to change my mind and not go to the gym, then I become out of integrity with the truth because I clearly said "Yes, I will go to the gym today." If I am unsure if I will be able to work out, I will usually tell others of my plans with more care by saying, "I will be going to the gym if I have the time. Today might be a busy day." This allows me to say out loud what I really mean, and that is that I am unsure if I will go. By the way, when you say that you will "try" to go to the gym, you might as well say, "No, I doubt I will go." You either are going or you are not going.

Parents, Teachers and Teenagers:

Think about how you speak to others. Do you clearly convey your truths, or are you wishy-washy? Below you are given a scenario of an athlete who goes against his values. Look at the solution and think about times you may have been out of integrity with your own values.

Think about Your Values

Imagine someone who has impeccable health, let's say, a teen basketball player. He needs to eat well, train hard, and rest the night before games to maintain a healthy, strong body that performs while he is playing on the court. If his goal was to score fifty points in the Saturday night basketball game against his rival team, it would not make sense if he went against his values and went to a party the night before the game and ate poorly, drank, smoked cigarettes, and stayed up late.

Parents and Teachers:

1. **What is the appropriate way to communicate to the athlete that he has disregarded his values in this situation?**

2. **Do you find it difficult to communicate your values to this person? Why or why not?**

3. **How do you overcome your difficulty and have clear communication about values and athletics?**

Possible Ways to Discuss Values:

The best way to communicate with someone about his or her values is to have clear and open communication.

Follow these steps:

1. Use your listening skills when you ask your teen athlete why he made the choice to go against his values and ended up not performing to the best of his ability at the game?

2. Watch your body language and aim to understand, not criticize, your teen.

3. Treat your teen with respect and do not judge him. Remember that you were once a teen and might have made similar choices.

4. Be precise about what you expect from your teen and tell him what you think he expects of himself.

5. Create clear guidelines and have solid consequences for not following them. Be ready to follow through on the consequences.

Teenagers: Imagine that you were the teen who disregarded his values by staying out late at a party. What can you do to get through this situation when you speak with your parents or your coach, who questions your choice?

1. Keep the lines of communication open. Explain to your parents or coach what made you make the poor decision. By explaining as much as you can, you can answer other questions your parent or coach might posed in an attempt to understand your actions.

2. Be respectful with your communication, both verbal and nonverbal.

3. Listen to what your parent or coach says.

4. Communicate how you feel by saying "This makes me feel…"

5. Express your desire to make amends, and come to a resolution.

Review

1. When you read the steps for developing self-motivation, what area did you realize you needed to work on the most?

   _____

   _____

   _____

   _____

   _____

2. Are you good at beginning projects? Do you finish what you start?

   _____

   _____

   _____

   _____

   _____

3. What can you do to improve your motivation?

   _____

   _____

   _____

   _____

   _____

4. What values are most important to you?

   _____

   _____

   _____

   _____

   _____

5. How do you see yourself? Would you be open to honest feedback from a close friend or family member so you can improve yourself?

_____

_____

_____

_____

_____

Extension
Exercise

Test yourself to see how motivated you are. Choose a small goal,
like cleaning your house, and see if you can follow through and accomplish that goal without procrastinating. Do you get an urge to
watch television, talk on the phone, or even go and make yourself a
cup of coffee? Discuss how readily you accomplished your task.

For Parents and Teachers:

How can you assist your children or students to follow through on a task?

Consider the following:

Offer rewards for completing the task. Find out what would motivate the child, and offer a good reward for a job well done. Parents can offer the car for the weekend, if their teen is demonstrating results with their school work.

Please note:

- You must explain to your teen that the task will not go away until it is completed.

- Do not enable your teen by completing the task for him or her or by ignoring that the teen has not completed the task.

- Help your teen to create a schedule to help him or her complete tasks.

- Provide positive incentives.

- Monitor results.

Test Your Current Knowledge of Self-Image

Teenagers, parents, and teachers: The image you hold of yourself is very often the way others see you as well. If you think you are a worthy individual and treat yourself with care and respect, by Law, others will also treat you with care and respect. If someone does not treat you the way you think you deserve to be treated, you would need to let that person know that you refuse to be the victim of their poor behavior.

1. What does it mean to you to have a positive self-image?

_____

_____

_____

_____

_____

_____

_____

_____

2. Do you think your thinking can affect your self-image? Why or why not?

_____

_____

_____

_____

_____

_____

_____

_____

3. Do you think that your subconscious thoughts can affect your body and how you carry yourself? Explain.

    _____

    _____

    _____

    _____

    _____

    _____

    _____

    _____

    _____

4. If you believe your thoughts can affect your body, could they also affect your finances, relationships, results at work, and the rest of your life? Explain.

    _____

    _____

    _____

    _____

    _____

    _____

    _____

    _____

    _____

Think
About This!

- Parents and teachers, think about how you view of yourself. Do you think and know you are incredible at what you do? Your self-image will determine the path that you will take in life, as it will be up to you to show others of your worth. Having a strong self-image means that no one can knock you off course with your goals by telling you "There is no way that will ever work!"

Did you know that the late Walt Disney took Art Linkletter to an open field near Orange County, California, pointed to the land, and told Linkletter of his dream of building a dream park for children? When asked if Linkletter would partner up with Disney for this venture, Linkletter said no.

He could not see Disney's dream. He even laughed at the idea of turning an orange field into a theme park. Had Disney not had such a positive self-image, he might have been affected by his friend's disbelief. He may have never moved forward with his idea to create Disneyland. Linkletter now preaches that:

"Be careful before you say no to any business offer."

Canadian-born Art Linkletter hosted of two of the longest-running television shows in United States broadcast history.

- Teenagers and students, your self-image will be the key in all that you move toward in your future. You have to believe and trust in yourself and your abilities in order for others to believe in you. Once you have mastered this skill, you will be well on your way to accomplishing any task you desire.

Lesson

Congratulations, you have done a considerable amount of work on yourself from the inside out, and I am sure that you have a better understanding of the areas of your life where you would like to see changes. You can apply the information you have learned here when you are having any sort of life challenge or problem.

Take Self Image for example. What comes to mind when you think about yourself? Are you thinking, "I am a beautiful person with infinite intelligence?" Or are you thinking about and focusing your attention on negative thoughts about yourself? Your results all begin with the thoughts you are thinking in your mind.

Let's take a closer look at just how important your thoughts are to your self-esteem and results in everyday life. We all have flaws; no one is perfect. However, it is easy to understand why we as a society expect ourselves to be perfect, especially when we compare ourselves to overexposed celebrities. If you were to ask, you would learn that a lot of airbrushing that takes place before a model's photos are put in print, and thick makeup is often applied before an actor shoots a scene for television.

Subconscious Mind

Remember the picture of your conscious and subconscious mind.

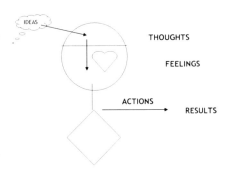

What does our self-image have to do with our results in life? I would say

198

everything. If we are confident with who we are, regardless of the fact that we might have a scar on our face or our body is not shaped like the women we see on television, we will walk with an air of confidence. If we walk with an air of confidence, we will change our level of vibration and begin to attract new, positive things. Once we begin to attract new and exciting things into our life, we begin to change our conditions, circumstances, and environment. This all happens because we changed the thoughts we were thinking of ourselves.

It all started with the conscious mind, which actively thinks a thought. This thought is then transferred to the subconscious mind, where we attach an emotion to the thought. Finally, the thought coupled with an emotion creates a result. If a thought creates a good emotion, then we will move towards our goals. If the thought creates a bad emotion, our guidance system is telling us that our thoughts will take us further from the joy or we are looking to create.[1]

When we repeatedly tell ourselves something for at least ninety days, we create a habit. Once we create a habit, this idea will be impressed on the subconscious mind; only then will our results change. Just think: if you are able to change your self-image, you can also improve your finances, relationships, sales goals, and grades for teenagers.

---

1   Hicks, Abraham Special Subjects 1, San Antonio, TX, Abraham-Hicks Publishers, 1989.

Review

 Think about The Law of Attraction and Vibration. Remember that your thoughts, even those that are only present in your subconscious mind, will put you in a certain vibration to attract only those concepts on the same vibration. If you are thinking thoughts such as, "I am so fat," you will not be on the right vibration to attract thoughts of health and the thinness that you desire. The key to changing any belief is to be happy exactly where you are. If you would like to change your weight, then you need to believe in your conscious and subconscious mind that you are first of all happy with the weight that you are currently at. You will have a feeling of gratitude for the body that you were given and the things that you are able to do with your body. Once you are grateful, your level of vibration changes. Then you must begin to act on what you desire.

To demonstrate your understanding of the mind, I would like to see if you can explain how a people can change their self-image, which in turn changes their self-esteem, which in turn changes every result in their lives.

1. Explain how it is possible to create negative conditions, negative circumstances, and a negative environment simply by thinking negative thoughts, even if those thoughts are in your subconscious mind.

_____

_____

_____

_____

2. Explain how you can create a positive condition, a positive circumstance, or a positive environment simply by changing your thoughts.

_____

_____

_____

_____

_____

_____

_____

_____

_____

_____

Extension
Exercises

How can you apply this same concept to other problems? Be sure to take into account the fact that wishful thinking is not all it takes to turn around serious problems.

1. **Financial problems**

_____
_____
_____
_____
_____
_____
_____

2. **Relationship problems**

_____
_____
_____
_____
_____
_____
_____

3. **Problems with grades**

_____
_____
_____
_____
_____
_____
_____

4. Worries about successfully performing your job

_____

_____

_____

_____

_____

_____

_____

Test Your Current Knowledge of Courage

Here you are face-to-face with your goals. Some of them may really terrify you. This is normal. Anything you have really wanted for a long time should have some fear attached to it. How are you going to jump past this fear and step into a world where happiness and joy await you?

- Parents and teachers, think about a time in your life when you were afraid to do something, but you knew you had to bite the bullet and do it anyway. Think about where you would be in life if you had not taken charge of what you really wanted, even though it might have been very uncomfortable.

- Teenagers and students, there will be times that you will need to rely on that magical power—courage—that you have inside you. Don't be afraid.

1. **What is courage, and do you think you have it? Why, or why not?**

_____

_____

_____

_____

2. **Have you ever done something that scared you to pieces, but you did it anyway? What were the results of this action?**

_____

_____

_____

_____

3. What happens to you when you face your fears?

_____

_____

_____

_____

4. Do you think there is a fine line between being courageous and being irresponsible? Explain.

_____

_____

_____

_____

5. Name some avoidance strategies you use when you face fear.

_____

_____

_____

_____

6. What does implementing avoidance strategies do to your goals?

_____

_____

_____

_____

LESSON NINE

How can you let your courage emerge from within and rocket your life?

Think
About This!

- Parents and teachers, when you thought about a time in your life when you had to be courageous in order to advance toward your goals, what did you remember? What kinds of things were holding you back from moving forward?

- Teenagers and students, as you move toward your goals, you are going to enter unchartered territory. Things will be scary and sometimes very uncomfortable. There is a price to pay for the success you desire, and most people will stop moving forward at the first sign of a challenge. When you are progressing toward a place you have never been before, know that it will feel uncomfortable. Expect it, and you will be well prepared to move past it.

Lesson

What is courage?

Without courage you will never move up or forward in life. You will become a self-absorbed weakling. Think outside of yourself, and see that there is more to life than the pain you feel as you move toward your goals. You must face this pain, and move on toward an exciting, fulfilled life.

> You gain strength, courage, and confidence by every experience in which you really stop to look fear in the face. You must do the thing which you think you cannot do.
> *Eleanor Roosevelt (1884–1962), first lady of the United States from 1933 to 1945.*

> Courage is not the absence of fear, but rather the judgment that something else is more important than fear.
> *Ambrose Redmoon (1933–1996), writer and manager of a rock band.*

> Courage is resistance to fear, mastery of fear—not absence of fear.
> *Mark Twain (1835–1910), American writer and lecturer.*

Most people will live their lives according to routine and safety. Who do you know who lives this way?

_____

_____

_____

_____

Abraham Maslow said, "Either step forward into growth or back to safety."

Life is all about facing your fears and experiencing growth. When you take a huge step toward something, there is a lot of fear. When you take little steps there is little fear.

Review

1. When have you felt fear?

_____

_____

_____

_____

_____

_____

2. You definitely want to associate with courageous people because it feels good to hang out with them. Who do you know who is courageous? Why do you find them courageous?

_____

_____

_____

_____

_____

_____

You must live the way you want to live, not the way you think you must settle for. Choose carefully as you have one chance to live your life. It will be not fun to have regrets later in life.

Remember, there is a fine line between being courageous and being irresponsible. You must replace self-pity with courage. When courage is lost, all is lost. The person who never has the courage to begin a task is the person who is destined to lose.

Extension
Exercise

Activity to Build Your Courage

1. In order to move past your fears, you first need to acknowledge
    what they are. Write a list of the Top Ten Things you would
    like to do, but you are afraid to do them.

    1.

    2.

    3.

    4.

    5.

    6.

    7.

    8.

    9.

    10.

2. How do you plan to use courage to move toward your goals?

_____

_____

_____

_____

_____

_____

_____

3. What will you do when fear confronts you?

_____

_____

_____

_____

_____

_____

_____

Visualize
Your Dreams

Visualizing your goals is a top secret skill that athletes have historically used for refined success in their sport. It is also a commonly practiced strategy with powerful business people who are regular goal achievers. Imagine that with daily practice, you also can have access to this skill.

Lesson

How does it work?

1. The more you can impress your goals and dreams on the subconscious mind, the faster you will attract your desires. Over time, your conscious mind will start to believe what you are telling it, and you will begin to bring your goals into physical form. Remember The Law of Physical Manifestation.

2. When you add emotion to visualization, you speed up the process of attaining your goals. If you want to go away on vacation to a beach somewhere, it is important to visualize the ocean and use your senses. Feel the sun on your face, smell the fresh ocean air, and even display some beach photos to help you turn your vision into reality. Make your vision as real as possible.

3. Expect your vision to come true. With expectation comes faith. You must have faith that you will have what you desire.

4. You will now begin to attract people into your conditions, circumstances, and environment. In turn this will bring your desires closer to you. Be sure to remain aware of your environment. You may face many everyday signals that will assist you as you strive to attain your vision. Maybe an advertisement comes across the radio for a special trip offer, but you can only take advantage of the discounted price if you take advantage of the sale that day. You need to be aware in order to receive these hints. If you're not paying attention, it will take a bit longer for your goal to come into physical form.

5. The more you visualize your goals, the more invested you become in your vision. You will become in harmony or resonance with what you really want. Emotion is our greatest motivator.

Review

Three Levels of Vision

Be:

Q- What do you want to *be* in life?

A- I am an enthusiastic person who inspires others to accomplish their goals.

Do:

Q- What do you want to *do* with your life?

A- I want to motivate ten million youth worldwide to accomplish their goals and dreams by taking accountability for their actions.

Have:

Q- What is your vision, your goal, or your end result?

A- This is what you need to figure out, so you can find purpose and meaning in your life.

It's Not About What You Have in Life, it's About What You Become

1. What do I want to be?

   _____

   _____

   _____

2. What do I want to do?

   _____

   _____

   _____

3. What do I want to have?

   _____

   _____

   _____

You must visualize yourself already in possession of that which you desire. It works best if you focus on what you can give to others, and not on how great you are. Take your attention off yourself and put it on others.

Extension
Exercise

1. **Create a vision board.**

Once you know what you want to *be, do,* and *have,* the next step is to create a vision board of pictures you connect with. There are a few ways that you can create a vision board. One way is to use pictures that you cut out of magazines. Find pictures of people you would like to be like. What are some things that you would like to do? Paste them on your board. What are some things you would like to have? Post the vision board in a place where you will see it daily.[1]

2. **Create an affirmation statement to go with each vision.**

   I am so happy and grateful now that—

3. **Expectation will bring your goals to you. Once you are repeating your affirmations for ninety days, they will become habit, and you will begin to attract your goals based on The Law of Attraction and Vibration.**

Be sure that you are surrounding yourself with positive people so your subconscious mind stays positive as you move toward your goals.

---

1 Go to achievemyvision.com for a revolutionary way to create your own vision board online. This is another proven method to create a path to your future while using technology.

Test Your Current Knowledge of What You Want to Do with the Rest of Your Life

We are entering the final stages of your study program. This lesson will help you take all you have learned and start to think about your higher purpose here on Earth. By this point, you should have a solid understanding of who you are, and you should clearly understand the values that are important in your life. The final step to the program is to figure out, "What do you want to do with the rest of your life?" This is a powerful question that many people ponder. How do you find this answer? You must take everything you have learned about yourself, and find what you are really passionate about. Turning this into a vocation might take some extra work and training on your behalf, but wouldn't it be worth it to end up doing something with your life that brings you excitement and joy each day?

Keep in mind that once you figure out what you want to do, you will need some help getting there. Because you cannot promote yourself, you will need to find three or four people to help you launch your idea to millions. Third-party credibility will be the key to launching your ideas to the world, and it will assist you in attaining your dreams. Who will be on your dream team?

- Parents and teachers, think about the path of life you have chosen for yourself. I know that sometimes life just happens, and we don't always end up doing the things we dreamed of. Maybe child rearing got in your way of pursuing your teaching degree. Or maybe you ended up in a career that pays well and enables you to provide very well for your family, but you are rarely home to see them. If you love what you do, that's great, keep living in the joy. However, if you have started to wish your life was different, just know that it is never too late to pursue the career of your dreams. This is especially true now that online education is so popular. You live your life only once. There are no second chances. If there is something you wish you could be doing, take the action steps necessary to move toward it. Don't just sit there and whine about it. Doug Wead on his *Power Mentor CD Program* reminds us to "get up and do something!"[1]

- Teenagers and students, you have your whole life to discover what you really want to do. Did you know that, according to Bob Proctor, "the average person works a total of twelve different jobs in five vocations before they figure out what they really want to do?" (*The Science of Getting Rich* seminar). The exciting part here is that as a teen, your future is wide open. Dream away, and dream big. You will be amazed at where you end up.

How do you want to be remembered, and what impact do you want to have on the world?

_____

_____

_____

_____

_____

_____

_____

_____

_____

_____

_____

_____

_____

_____

_____

_____

_____

_____

1   Wead, Doug, *The Power Mentor*, Audio CD, 2000.

LESSON TEN

What Difference Will You Make in Your Lifetime?

Think
About This!

- Parents and teachers, this last lesson will allow you to reflect on your life and make decisions about your future. Are you on the path of your dreams, or is there something else you would like to be doing with your life? Think about the legacy you would like to leave of yourself for others as well as your family. Are you living life to the max?

- Teenagers and students, this section will help you reach some conclusions about your future. Think about some of the things that are important to you and how you would like to make a difference. You really can make a difference.

Lesson

Now that you have taken a closer look at how you conduct your life, how you think, what your values are, and what is important to you, you must realize that you have a good start on most people. When asked, most people have no idea what they value let alone, what change they want to make in the world.

> Be the change you want to see in the world.
> *Gandhi (1869–1948), political*
> *and spiritual leader of India.*

1. **How do you want to be remembered in a thousand years?**

_____

_____

_____

_____

_____

_____

_____

_____

2. **Do you know anyone who is out of integrity? Explain.**

_____

_____

_____

_____

_____

_____

_____

_____

3. How do most people feel about people like who are out of integrity?

_____

_____

_____

_____

_____

_____

_____

_____

4. Do you know someone who "walks their talk?"

_____

_____

_____

_____

_____

_____

_____

_____

5. Are you careful about being in integrity with what you say?

_____

_____

_____

_____

_____

_____

_____

Inspiring Stories of People Who Gave Back to Help Others

The whole idea of creating a plan for you is for the end result—being able to give back to others. Here are some incredible stories from www.JustGive.Org about some inspiring people who gave back to others before thinking of themselves.

I have tried to teach people that there are three kicks in every dollar: one, when you make it—and how I love to make a dollar; two, when you have it—and I have the Yankee lust for saving. The third kick is when you give it away—and it is the biggest kick of all.

William Allen White (1868–1944),
American newspaper editor, politician, and author

A person's true wealth is the good he or she does in the world.

Mohammad

Forklift Operator Opens his Heart and Donates Over $1 Million to Charity

"Mat" Dawson, a forklift driver at Ford Motor Co. donated $200,000 to Wayne State University in Detroit, Michigan for, scholarships. The gift brings to over $1 million the total amount Dawson has donated to charity so far.
When asked what motivated him to give, Dawson said, "I was raised like that—to help others… I enjoy it… I just want people to say that I tried to help somebody."[1]

Think about who you know who gives back to society and to others, often ahead of themselves. These people are like real live angels, who are looking out for the well being of others, instead of themselves. These people are very rare, as we have been taught to be "go-getters" not "go-givers." A small shift in thinking can make a huge difference to someone else's life.

Think about who you can give to today! Now, go out and do it.

---

1 *Philanthropy News Digest* (Vol. 5, Issue 15, April 14, 1999).

Review

Now that you have had a chance to think about what you would like to do with the rest of your life, go back to your visualization lesson and get to work believing in your vision. This will take time and practice, but you will eventually draw everything you desire to you.

Since I have been working on my mind, I have kept a vision board over my desk. When the items on the board materialize, I check them off. I recently noticed that the things that I wanted ten years ago are still on my vision board today, as many of them are things that I always want. For example, I love walks on the beach, so each year, I envision that I will spend some time walking along a beach, listening to the waves crashing on the rocks, and smelling the salt in the air. I always want to enjoy my exercise, sleep well, and be healthy, so I continue to envision myself living in a healthy body.

Take a close look at your vision board and see what things hold the most importance to you. You can learn a lot about yourself from your vision board.

Extension
Exercises

When you take a close look at the vision board you have created, you will clearly see whether you are heading in the direction of your dreams. Your vision board is your plan, so if you see something that you would like to change over time, all you need to do is either add it to or remove it from the board.

PART THREE

Putting it All Together: A Master Plan for a Better Life

Prepare

- Parents and teachers, as you answer these questions, think about the changes you want to make in your lives. Are you on the right path? Do you know what you would like to do with your life? Do you have all the pieces you need to make yourself a success? What areas do you need to work on? Remember that anything worthwhile will take time, effort, and persistence, but will be well worth it.

- Teenagers and students, as you answer these questions, you are creating an action plan for areas that you might need to work on. Take note on the areas that you think you need to focus on, and then spend some time on this lesson. You can always do more research at your local library or online.

Think
About This!

Now is your chance to put together all the different parts of this program to create a plan for your future. See how many of these questions you can answer without looking back at your notes.

Lesson 1:
Attitude

Write out some concepts of a winning attitude. We know that it takes at least ninety days to change a habit. Focus on these three concepts for ninety days, and see how your results change.

1.

2.

3.

Lesson 2: Your Mind and the Six Higher Faculties

When working or going about your day, think about all that you do using your conscious mind and all of the times you are operating with your subconscious mind. Give some examples of each.

Conscious thinking:

1.

2.

3.

Subconscious thinking:

1.

2.

3.

Don't forget that strengthening your six higher faculties of the mind just takes practice. Find some books at your local library on this topic, and take your practice a step further by spending one evening a week concentrating on your higher faculties. Do this instead of doing something you used to do that does not exercise your mind. (Watching television does not strengthen your mind).

Lesson 3: The Laws of the Universe

Practice The Law of Vibration and Attraction to see what you can bring into your life.

1. How well did you do with attracting the three things you really want? Explain your results.

_____

_____

_____

_____

_____

_____

When difficult times confront your life, see if you can find some answers with The Laws of the Universe.

2. Explain a situation when you were able to obtain a deeper understanding because of your knowledge of the laws. Also, outline how you were able to move through the situation. Be sure to specify which law you used: Attraction/Vibration, Polarity, Rhythm, Relativity, Cause and Effect, or Physical Manifestation.

_____

_____

_____

_____

_____

_____

Lesson 4: Goal Setting and Persistence

Go back to your list of twenty-five immediate goals and narrow them down to just ten. Start working immediately on these goals. See the movie *The Bucket List* (2008) starring Morgan Freeman and Jack Nicholson to get some incentive for your motivation to move forward.

My List of Ten Immediate Goals:

1.

2.

3.

4.

5.

6.

7.

8.

9.

10.

Are you persistent enough to achieve your goals? Explain.

Lesson 5:
Confidence

What is your confidence formula, and are you repeating it every day? Write your affirmation here:

_____

_____

_____

_____

_____

_____

Lesson 6:
Responsibility

How well do you think you take responsibility? Give an example.

_____

_____

_____

_____

_____

_____

_____

Lesson 7: Understanding Your Paradigms, or Habits

What goal did you write down as the goal that you are too afraid to go after? If you really want this goal, explain how you plan to blast through the terror barrier to achieve it.

_____
_____
_____
_____
_____
_____
_____

Lesson 8: Self-Motivation,
Your Values, and Self-Image

1. What helps you motivate yourself?

   _____

   _____

   _____

2. What values are most important to you?

   _____

   _____

   _____

   _____

3. What happens when you start to take action to achieve your goals?

   _____

   _____

   _____

   _____

4. Do you have a good self-image? Explain.

   _____

   _____

   _____

5. What steps do you need to do to move toward your goals without interruptions?

   _____

   _____

   _____

Lesson 9:
Courage

Did you overcome your top-ten fears?

To move past your fears, you first need to acknowledge what they are. Write a list of the top-ten things that you would like to do if you weren't afraid to do them.

1.

2.

3.

4.

5.

6.

7.

8.

9.

10.

It's Not About What You Have in Life, it's What You Become

What do you want to become?

What I want to be:

_____
_____
_____
_____

What I want to do:

_____
_____
_____
_____

What I want to have:

_____
_____
_____
_____

Lesson Ten: What Difference Will You Make in Your Lifetime?

How do you want to be remembered in a thousand years?

_____
_____
_____
_____
_____
_____
_____
_____
_____
_____
_____
_____
_____
_____
_____
_____
_____
_____
_____
_____
_____
_____
_____
_____
_____
_____

Congratulations on Completing
The Secret for Teens Revealed!

Think
About This!

- Parents and teachers, I know that if you understand these concepts and implement them into your own life, you will see results. There will be times when you will want to give up because making significant changes in your life does take effort, persistence, and time. These lessons are a gift that you can use for yourself, as well as with others. I hope you have enjoyed your time studying with me, and know that the results you will achieve will make this study worth your while.

- Teenagers and students, I want to stress how lucky you are to have access to this material. I have watched hundreds of teens advance quickly toward their goals by using these concepts. If you take this program seriously and complete all the activities, you will live the life you think you can only have in your dreams.

Personal Reflection from the Author

My life changed very quickly back in 1996 when I picked up Bob Proctor's book *You Were Born Rich*. From that book, I learned that I had unlimited potential, and I set out to use it. I think back now, and I am so grateful for the path I have chosen.

It's been quite a trip since then, but I am amazed at how my life has changed from that moment, more than twelve years ago, when I was first introduced to these concepts. As you can see from the preface, there are so many places where you can gather answers as you continue on this path of study.

Remember the key to *The Secret for Teens Revealed* will be persistent action. Your biggest goals will only seem huge to you in your mind, but in someone else's mind, they may seem very simple. It is you who will determine your results in life, and it is only you who can make things happen for yourself. Do not forget that there is a big difference between knowing these concepts, and actually putting them into practice.

There were times when I thought about giving up on my dreams, but the thoughts only lasted a few seconds. I would bask in self-doubt and then move on from it because I knew that I had more belief in myself.

I will only say to you, "dream big," and enjoy every moment you have. Life can be such an adventure.

My best,
Andrea Samadi

Acknowledgments

The following people helped make this work possible. Without all their efforts, this project would still be sitting on the bottom of my bookshelf. I would like to thank:

Majid Samadi for attending PSI Principia with me, studying Bob Proctor's SGR Program with me, and being there every step of the way as I moved toward my dreams;

Hazel and Frank MacPhail for understanding my need to leave the teaching profession to study personal development back in 1997. Thanks for supporting me while I pursued my dreams of living in the United States;

Christine Gallant and Karen Volk: for being such great big sisters, and listening to my dreams, no matter how crazy they seemed to be. Your love and support has always been felt and appreciated;

Anita and Rolf Wieland: for their continued support and kindness while showing me by example how to live up to my highest potential;

Mark Low: for teaching me how to sell and showing me that it can also be fun;

Pixie Low: for keeping me focused on my dreams and asking when I planned to make them realities;

Linda and Bob Proctor: for being such incredible mentors. I will be forever grateful to have had the opportunity to work with Bob Proctor's Youth Mentor International, where my soul was touched for a lifetime. Thanks for all that you have taught me;

3% Club Mastermind Group Team: consisting of Carla Fryling, Linda Ware, Barbara Gay, and Shirley Krevinghaus. Thanks for keeping my pulse going in the time since we met and wrote our first book together in 2001. An honorable mention goes to Alice Meehan;

Sandy Rogers: for her support and assistance as I wrote the first edition of this program in 2002. I would also like to thank her for being such a help when I first moved to the United States;

Margaret Merrill: for being an incredibly supportive and loving lifelong friend whom I am thankful I met at Bob Proctor's SGR Seminar in 1999;

Jim Carson: for always reminding me that I could return to teaching;

Pearson Education: for allowing me the opportunity to work with resourceful managers as well as the NovaNET Team. Special thanks to Jennifer Sikora and Joni Schlapa for brainstorming ideas with me;

Easter Seals Leaders of Tomorrow Program: for providing me with an opportunity to work with many talented young adults who made a lasting impact on my life.

Dr. James Jorgenson and Squaw Peak Dental: for holding me accountable to my personal goals. Who would think your dentist would hold you accountable to your personal goals!?

The original twelve YMI teens for inspiring me to write this material: Scot and Jim Keranen, Ashley Nelson, Ryan Tara, Michael Sanson, Brian Johnson, Matt Weins, Justin Tanas, Heather Cunningham, Nathaniel Eborn, Jen Marvin and Sara Peccianti;

Maria Cesnik: for allowing me to bounce ideas off her as well as for being a lifelong friend;

Gerry Robert: who taught me powerful information in his *Publish-*

ing for Profits seminar and guided me in the right direction with this book;

Camelback Mountain Regular Hikers: for saying, "hello," and keeping me motivated all these years;

Patti Knoles: for helping me design this book's cover and for being there when I first moved to Arizona;

Susan Wenger and the Wheatmark Publishing Team: for helping me to create the final revisions with this book.

In Memory of Successful CEO of Webfeat Multimedia

The book was written in memory of my friend Christian Gerard (1970–2007), founder of Webfeat Multimedia of Toronto, Canada.

Christian's passion for life, his family and friends, and his ongoing commitment to personal success truly made him a unique individual. He will always be remembered as a dynamic entrepreneur who lived his short thirty-six years to the fullest. In memory of Christian, please do not forget to live in the moment every day and enjoy your life; you never know when it will be your time.

Bibliography

Abraham, Jay. *Getting Everything You Can Out of All You've Got.* New York, New York: St. Martin's Press, 2000.

Barker, Joel. *Paradigms: The Business of Discovering the Future.* New York, New York, Harper Collins 1992.

Byrne, Rhonda. *The Secret.* TS Production LLC, 1996.

Canfield, Jack. *Self-Esteem and Peak Performance*, audio CD. Overland Park, Kansas. CareerTrack, 1990.

Dyer, Wayne. *There is a Spiritual Solution to Every Problem.* New York, New York: Harper Collins, 2003.

Frankl, Viktor. *Man's Search for Meaning*, Boston: Beacon Press, 2006.

Gardner, Howard. *Frames of Mind.* New York, New York: Basic Books, 1983.

Gove, Bill. *The Ultimate Speaking Package*, DVD. Boynton Beach, Florida: Gove-Siebold.

Guan, Joseph. *Energy Psychology* seminar, 2002.

Hansen, Mark Victor. *101 Goals*, speech at the 3% Club seminar, 2000.

———. *How to Think Bigger than You Ever Thought You Could Think,* audio book. Provo, UT, Enlightened Millionaire Institute, 2003.

Hawkins, David. R. *Power vs. Force: The Hidden Determinants of Human Behavior.* Sedona, Arizona: Veritas Publishing, 1995.

Hicks, Jerry and Esther. *Special Subjects Volume 1.* San Antonio, Texas: Abraham-Hicks Publishers, 1989.

Hill, Napoleon. *Think and Grown Rich.* London, England: Penguin Books Ltd., 2003.

Holliwell, Raymond. *Working With the Law: 11 Truths for Successful Living.* DeVorse and Co., 2005.

Murphy, Joseph. *Power of Your Subconscious Mind.* Radford, Virginia: Wilder Publications, 2008.

Proctor, Bob. *You Were Born Rich.* Scottsdale, Arizona: LifeSuccess Productions, 1984.

————. *The Success Puzzle: How to Find the Missing Pieces to Living Your Ideal Life,* audio cassette. Steamboat Springs, Colorado: LifeSuccess Productions, 1998.

————. *The Science of Getting Rich Seminar.* Cartersville, Georgia: LifeSuccess Productions, 1996.

————. *Success Series: Bob Proctor's 12 Power Principles*, audio cassettes. Toronto, Ontario, Canada: Bob Proctor Communications International Corp., 1993.

PSI Seminars, (Basic Seminar, PSI 7 Seminar, Women's Leadership Seminar, PLD Seminar, and Principia Seminar). PSI Ranch, Clearlake Oaks, California.

Friends of the Renaissance. *Living in Harmony by Natural Law,* Salt Lake City: Envision Press, 2001.

Tolle, Eckhart. *The Power of Now: A Guide to Spiritual Enlightenment.* Canada: Namaste Publishing, 1999.

Wead, Doug. *The Power Mentor Audio CD Program and Workbook*, audio CD. 2000.

Lightning Source UK Ltd.
Milton Keynes UK
UKOW04f1842130214

226440UK00001B/71/P